John Rankin Rogers

Politics

An argument in favor of the inalienable rights of man

John Rankin Rogers

Politics
An argument in favor of the inalienable rights of man

ISBN/EAN: 9783337134372

Printed in Europe, USA, Canada, Australia, Japan

Cover: Foto ©Suzi / pixelio.de

More available books at **www.hansebooks.com**

POLITICS

An Argument in Favor of the Inalienable
Rights of Man.

—By—

John R. Rogers

With an introduction by
Salmon M. Allen

·

INTRODUCTION.

THE effort to substitute reason for force in human government has not been many times seriously attempted in the history of the race, and has been successful in very few instances. Man's development began with his physical or animal nature, and it was but natural therefore, that the attempt at government should have assumed at first the character of force. With the development of the intellect has come a rebellion against a government of force, and a longing for one based upon reason. But the development of the reason, though making immense strides in the 5000 years of the world's history, has had to struggle hard against the mere animal in man ; and looking back from the heights of this closing scene of the 50th century it still looks as if the mere animal was yet in the ascendency, and that the race had not yet secured for itself the domination of its reason in matters governmental, much less the domination of its spiritual nature. The race is thinking hard, but it thinks largely along the lines of its animal parts, and we have as a result, government based on force with the selfishness of the animal in the ascendancy.

In our own land, for a century and a fraction we have been groping around to find some method of getting our reason on top, and holding the animal in subjection. Instinctive justice and our partly educated spiritual nature have made an effort to substitute reason in the government of our people. It has been however, but a halting, lame attempt, and the century is about to close with the experiment only a half success and the dread of a total failure impending like a gloomy cloud over us, while over the larger part of the world the race is still subservient to a government of force. Reason alone seems wholly inadequate to the struggle; and even assisted by the "spark of divinity" within us for 2000 years, reaches this 50th cycle of time far from triumphant. But man in his full nature is persistent, progressive, determined and hopeful. The contest is one for the supremacy of the reason, but the reason kept in contact with the animal nature alone, if this were possible, amounts to little more than instinct, and will accomplish little beyond brute force in government. But reason, under the influence of the spiritual or Divine nature, may develope a power adequate to be substituted in all the relationships of life for brute force.

May it not be that what we call instinctive justice is the silent power of the Divinity within us, slumbering, in a sort of animal lethargy, and occasionally aroused to rebuke the selfishness of the mere animal.

May it not be that when this slumbering spark of Divinity gets into a blaze, that reason may be dazzled by its brilliancy, captivated by its cheer, and yield to its full control. If so, the reason may gain power over the animal, and give us a government in which selfish individualism may cease and a loving co-operation be substituted. When this becomes possible we may look for permanency in a government of the people by the people and for the people.

While this struggle for the supremacy of the Divinity within us is in progress it is cheering to find, even rarely, such a broad and logical argument as that from the pen of my esteemed friend embraced in the following pages. I have read it with deep interest. Its tendency is to strengthen the hope that it may yet be possible for the race to reach some fundamental, basic principles, which, enacted into constitutional law, may give us a government in which there may be at least better opportunity for the further development of the reason under the guide of our better nature. It would be well if we could have more such literature in politics. A political literature that appeals to the partisan as a partisan, tends rather to drag down than build up, is debasing not uplifting. Brother Rogers has been able to dig deep. He will stir the slumbering embers of the fires which God has kindled within us, which, it is to be hoped, will never be quenched. His appeal is to the higher nature, not from the standpoint of a partisan, but from the standpoint of a brother man, with a heart overflowing with a longing desire to see the race emancipated from the thralldom of force, and its inalienable rights and liberties intrenched behind constitutional law. The realization of his theories will go far to hasten the day when man shall peacefully submit himself to the government of his reason. That this day may not be in the dim distance, and that America may have the honor of initiating reason's first great triumph in government is the sincere wish of

Yours truly,

SALMON M. ALLEN.

POLITICS.

An argument in behalf of the inalienable rights of man.

—BY—

JOHN R. ROGERS

My father was a Democrat, and in his way, something of a politician. As a boy I heard the arguments of the Democrats, read Democratic newspapers and very naturally imbibed their notions regarding slavery and the tariff. I heard with much inward satisfaction the story of the disagreement of my paternal and maternal grandfathers, long before my birth in Jackson's time, upon the time-honored tariff question. More than sixty years ago one of these men pulled off his coat and announced his intention of "licking" the other because he did not believe in "free trade and sailors' rights." Descended from a Revolutionary "privateersman," I naturally took sides—in my mind—with the first, and during all my boyhood days regretted the fact that he did not carry out his threat. In this boyish frame of mind I imagined that if he had done so, at least one step would have been taken toward the proper settlement of a momentous question. The The opportunity passed unimproved and men still continue to quarrel.

Poor grandfather, he was ready to do battle in defence of the honor of his sailor father, old "Captain Jonny," but he couldn't settle the tariff matter. And now after sixty years of dispute, of which I know something, I begin to fear that the pecuniary interests of those who wish to impose tariff taxes and those who do not wish to pay them may be impossible of settlement. In all ages of the world I find that men have ever desired to impose upon other men the burden of their support, and that so far, in one way or another, a class of men have always been able, not only to do this but to make the vast majority think it right that it should be so.

It is true that there have always been a few who did not agree to this, who held with the Gallilean Teacher the essential brotherhood of man, with its necessary consequence — absence of special privilege—but the world has generally voted them "cranks" or "pestilent fellows," and usually gotten rid of them and the awkward questions they have asked, with scant ceremony.

In the spring of 1856 I started alone, a mere boy, to visit my relatives in the states of Mississippi and Louisiana. Arriving at Louisville I took passage on the palatial Mississippi river steamer Niagara, Capt. Harry Leathers, for Vicksburg. The Niagara was too large to come through the canal at Louisville and so lay at Portland, about three miles below. Taking a hack I soon found the steamer with a large crew busily engaged in loading for the voyage to New Orleans. Capt. Leathers and his chief clerk were very polite and explained to me that although it might be a day or two before the boat was ready to start, still, I was perfectly welcome to come aboard and remain until Vicksburg was reached.

Traveling in those days was more leisurely done than at present. The steamer in due time proceeded down the river, but long stops were made at various places to take on freight and passengers, and it thus happened that some seven or eight very pleasant days had passed before Vicksburg came in sight. Shut up together the passengers became in a short time quite well acquainted. At some landing in northern Mississippi there came aboard during the night a plain, kindly looking old gentleman who the next morning at breakfast happened to sit next to me. We fell into conversation and strange to say became in the three or four days which followed, quite intimate. He was some sixty years of age, plainly dressed, a planter, living on his plantation near Vicksburg, and apparently a man of strict integrity and moral uprightness. How this old gentleman came to take me as a "chum" it seems hard to determine except that neither of us drank, cursed, played cards or gambled. And as these seemed to be the principal occupations of the gentlemen aboard it may have been sufficient reason. Anyhow, I was much impressed with the old man; he seemed above the ordinary weakness and meanness of life, and gave me much information regarding the country to which I was bound, mixed with good advice and much generous reflection. Under these circumstances one can well believe that I was somewhat shocked on our arrival to see him go below and bring out from the freight deck a horse and saddle and a mullatto boy of about my own age. He had said nothing to me about this "property" and as he had came aboard in the night I had seen nothing of it. I sat on the passenger deck of the steamer, twelve or fifteen feet above them, and watched their preparations for departure. The boy was a "bright mullatto," clean looking and decent, but his face showed such misery that I instantly took his part—in my mind again. He was hand cuffed and I found had been chained up near his master's horse on the lower deck while the aforesaid master was giving me good advice in the grand saloon above. The master rather awkwardly explained to me that the boy had run away, that he had followed him many weary miles on horseback to the Tennessee line, had finally captured him and was now nearing home with his "property." After he had saddled his horse he unlocked and took off the hand cuffs, that the boy might have more freedom in walking, produced from his saddlebags a small rope, tied one end securely round this half grown boy's neck, got on his horse, tied the other end of the rope around the pummel of his saddle and with a chirrup to his horse they were off up that steep hill side.

I don't think the slave opened his mouth during all this time, but he "looked!" so broken hearted and discouraged. His whole story was in his eyes. This was my first introduction to "the peculiar institution" and for a moment I began to doubt its entire wisdom and justice, but other things distracted my attention and for the time the incident passed out of my mind. Afterward I wondered how so good an old man as the planter evidently was could be so cruel to one who likely enough might have been his own son, but I have since come to see that custom and pecuniary interest are sufficient to warp the minds of most men completely. Now-a-days our manner of doing business separates the cause from the effect by such a distance that most fail to note the relation between them. The money dealers by their management cause misery, failure, disease, crime and death with far greater certainty and more culpability than the slaveholders of the past, but most of them refuse to acknowledge it even to themselves. The distance between the cause and effect is a little greater, that is all. This slaveholder was a kind hearted man, naturally just, where "business" was not concerned, and so are large numbers of men chiefly responsible for the enormous misery of our cities today.

In 1860 I was a resident of Hinds county Mississippi. The war between the states was just then coming on. Preparations for its advent were to be seen on every hand. Leaders of secession were industriously engaged in fanning into flame the fires of sectional hatred. "Firing the southern heart," was the business of the time with them. Newspapers were filled, speeches made, all with one end in view. "We are not responsible for slavery," they said. "Our forefathers brought the negros here. The responsibility of caring for them is upon us. We shall feed and clothe them and they shall have religious instruction and want for nothing of which they really stand in need. Slavery is upheld by the Bible and the churches; but even if it were not, even if it is a sin, we will answer to God for that. We are not responsible to the consciences of our northern brothers. Local self-government is one of the distinctive features of our republic. We have a constitutional right to conduct our own affairs in our own way. The rights not expressly delegated to the general government remain with the states; this being expressly state dand understood at the time of the organization of our government and the ratification of the constitution, our only bond of union. We shall not go to the North to interfere with their forms of government or with their domestic institutions. We want to be let alone; to be allowed to manage our affairs in our own way and if in the wrong we will render account at least to the Judge of All. But if the north sends its armies to invade our states we will meet them as Tom Corwin said the Mexicans ought to receive the Americans in 1846, "We will welcome them with bloody hands to hospitable graves." They will then be invaders; we shall fight for our firesides and our homes; for all men hold dear. We do not invite the contest, but if forced upon us let it come; the responsibility be upon the heads of those who instigate war."

This is the way they talked in 1869 in the South. Their orators made the welkin fairly ring with their denunciations, one of their ablest men saying in substance: "Twelve millions of brave and determined people fighting in defence of their homes were never yet conquered by invading armies." And this was true—up to that time. Southern sympathizer as I was then, and for years afterward, I felt the force of this. I was inclined to think them wrong on the slavery question but absolutely right in their determination to secede from those states which persisted in the attempt to interfere with their right to local self-government.

Today I can see the weakness of their argument and the cause of their failure. It is easy now. True, they did fight for local self-government. They were brave and determined. They were united. But their weakness was this: *The foundation for which they fought was their ability to absorb the profits of other men's labor.* That was all they wanted. But it was too much. It was unjust, and the time had come for that particular form of slavery to die.

Today Mr. Pullman says to his men: "These works are mine, they belong to myself and my associates; they are my property. You do not even claim to own a single share of the stock. You can then have no rightful claim to interfere with my management of this property. I shall treat you fairly and shall pay you promptly. If you don't like my service you are free to leave it. But I must be free to manage my business in the way I choose. All I want is to be let alone in the management of what you concede is my property. If interfered with I shall let loose the dogs of war upon you. I have a right guaranteed by the laws of the land to do as I am doing and if you force me to fight I shall do so in defence of the dearest right of every citizen; to-wit: the right to acquire and hold property, a right without which civilization could not exist.

So far Mr. Pullman. Mr. Carnegie says the same and so say all the monopolists. In real truth, the thing that they will hire poor devils to kill other poor devils for, is, *that a system may live which enables them to absorb the profits of labor.* It is the old story over again. Slave-managers and slave-owners are one in sentiment and intent. Upon the robbery of labor they have grown great and magnificent. They have sworn that it shall continue. That is all they want. To be let alone—in the robbery of labor. But it is too much. It is unjust and the time is rapidly drawing near when this form of slavery, too, will die. Advancing intelligence and the ballot will make it impossible.

The United States census has some wonderful facts laid up for the inquirer. If the total production of wealth be divided by the number of days of labor done it will be seen that the production aggregates more than $10 for each day's work. But the average wage in the United States is only about $1.00.

All wealth is created by labor. Yet while labor creates $10 in wealth monopoly has announced its decision to bring on the army and "a stronger government" unless $9 out of each $10 be obsequiously handed over. The difference between this condition of affairs and chattel slavery I leave my readers to determine.

Professor Emile de Laveleye, an eminent student of historical politics, says:

No democracy can exist permanently if its people are in a state of marked material inequality. Voters who get from their labor a scanty living while others about them are rich will probably in the end seek to alter the laws that sanction inequality. The rich will support the laws and if necessary call in the aid of a dictator. So democracy terminates in either anarchy or despotism, and usually in one as the result of the other. Under such conditions inequality is the cause of its downfall. The social problem involved in this phenomenon troubles all nations.

Degradation the Inevitable Result of Privation.

In 1856 the only completed railroad, I think, in the state of Mississippi, was one of some fifty miles in length extending from Vicksburg east to Jackson, Hinds county, then, as now, the capital of the state. My uncle's plantation was some sixteen miles from Jackson, near the Copiah county line. Those who remember the political sensations of the "reconstruction" period will not soon forget Copiah and its bloody record. The cars upon this primitive railroad were very accommodating, stopping almost anywhere that a gentleman desired either to get on or off, and so after what seemed a long, long time I finally arrived at my destination. My uncle and his family received me warmly and welcomed me to the state. Although quite young I had had some years of previous experience as a clerk in the city of Boston and it so happened that after some time spent in visiting I secured a position in a store at Jackson. Jackson was only a country village in fact, though a city in name. It had some three or four thousand white inhabitants, and about the same number of blacks. Life passed very leisurely with these people then. Money was plenty, cotton brought a fair price and "niggers" were high.

I boarded with the Rev. Mr. ——, the pastor of the Presbyterian church and also the editor of the "Witness," the organ of the Presbyterians in the Southwest. Mr. —— was a tall, dark complexioned man, a native Mississippian and I believe a thoroughly good man. He had all the angularity and the quaintness of Abraham Lincoln, in fact he looked something like him. Among other property he owned a mulatto "boy," or man, named Tom, who used to pull the lever at the printing office. My store lay between the printing office and the house, so that it often happened that Tom came into my place of business on his way back and forth from the office to his meals. I was naturally curious regarding the relation of master and slave and it thus came about that Tom soon confided to me his troubles.

Tom was a young man and he had a young wife to whom he was very much attached. Indeed, so far as I could judge he thought as much of her as if he had not been black. She was a house servant belonging to another master and was principally engaged in caring for the small white children belonging to her master, who was then talking of moving from Jackson to one of his plantations on the Yazoo, some sixty miles away. The mere thought of this put poor Tom in agony. If thus separated it was regarded as final; such a separation being like death, it had no cure. Several times when his wife passed the store in charge of her master's little ones Tom hurried me to the door to see her, apparently for the purpose of proving that his description of her perfections was not overdrawn. Poor Tom, although a man of twenty-five, bright and intelligent, his complete helplessness made him, in some respects, a mere child.

Tom's wife was a peculiarly fine looking girl. Although quite dark, indeed almost black, there was evidently white blood in her veins, for her hair was long, exceedingly abundant and only slightly "wavy." Her features were of the Caucasian type and she carried herself in the proud, self-confidant, self-contained manner never seen among blacks of pure breed. Seemingly, she should have been white, or nearly so, but through

some strange reversion in breeding she was born with a black skin. Such cases were rare in the South, but all familiar with life there have met with similar instances. To say that Tom was proud of her would be putting it mildly indeed; he fairly doted on her; and all the time he feared he was about to lose her.

Put yourself in his place my friend. Do you say he was only a mulatto, ignorant and incapable of feeling? Ah, but he had more of this than most coldblooded sons of the north, and what he had, what he was, came from nature, from God, was his by right divine. Have a care dear sir in this, for if you by virtue of superior attainments can limit the right of those below you in the social or mental scale what shall prevent your limitation by those above you?

One day Tom came to me in tears. His eyes were bloodshot and he sunk down on a box in the store limp and disconsolate. "Da done taken her away," was all he could say. I tried to encourage him all I could, but to no purpose. He soon took himself off, a woe begone specimen surely.

After that, for a time, Tom did not come in but shuffled by, his eyes on the ground. I soon began to hear, from McGill, a young white man who worked in the office, of Tom's general worthlessness. He was: "Just no count at all." You couldn't put the least dependence upon him, and if reproved he became sullen and even "disrespectful." Evidently he needed a whipping, my informant thought; that would straigten him out. 'Twas the only way to handle niggers. But it wouldn't be worth while to hope for that, for Tom was one of the slaves left to Mr. —— by his father and he wouldn't have him whipped. But his master was going to give him "a talking to and threaten him good," for he had said he would. Some days afterward I called Tom in as he went by and the whole story came out, as I knew it would. His master had given him the "good talking to" promised, and told him that it was perfectly idle for him to grieve and "go on" so about that girl, that she was just as good as dead to him and that as he was a likely looking nigger he would have no trouble in getting another wife, just as good, and that if he didn't quit his foolishness that he, the master, would be obliged, much against his wishes to send him around to the calaboose and have him whipped.

"Dat man," said Tom, "he married me hisself to my wife, and (passionately) she is my wife. I hear him preach bout de ordinances of God, and he tell us God love all, bof black and white, jus de same. He mus tink I'm a fool. But my God, Marse John what kin I do? I jes wish I's diad, dat's what I do."

Poor Tom? There was little to be said, and I said it. Hope and the pursuit of happiness make up our lives, the lives of all the children of men. Take away this and what wonder that men become sullen and even "disrespectful." The other day I heard a comfortable citizen bemeaning a poor man with a large family, who, he said, wouldn't work. He was asked if he, the comfortable citizen, could furnish him work, and he acknowledged that he could not. Did he know of any one who could or would? And again he was obliged to confess that he did not. And I happened to know that this poor man, who was really fit for better things, was anxiously searching, without success, for an opportunity to toil in the most menial capacity, that thereby he might buy bread for his children. That the mortal pangs of fear of coming want had taken hold of his very life, he had confided to me. The family I knew. The children were bright and intelligent, and the parents were intensely anxious regarding their future. The mother struggled and pinched and worked at unwomanly tasks outside the home, that she might send them to school. And all seemingly to little purpose, for they were getting further and further behind, week after

week and month after month. For a year past the father had had work, never at more than a dollar a day, and now even that was gone. With nerves and muscles weakened and strained by toil and lack of proper food he was almost desperate. He was certainly despairing. What could he do? Why should he work? Life to him was a treadmill. Hope in the future was gone, even if the much sought for "work" was given him. Why should he struggle on, only to fail in life's purpose at last? With him the question was raised, so well stated by the poet:

To be, or not to be; that is the question;
Whether 'tis nobler in the mind to suffer
The slings and arrows of outrageous fortune,
Or to take up arms against a sea of troubles,
And by opposing end them?

The laws governing the science of mathematics are no surer in their operation than the laws controlling poor human nature. They are absolute and can not be infringed without suffering and consequent degradation; and who so assists, even in the remotest degree, in the degradation of "the image of God" let him tremble, for all the powers of earth and air are pledged to his punishment. Men and women must be able to hope. Some small gain must be theirs. "The pursuit of happiness," that inalienable right of man, must not be made impossible.

But who is to blame for the unchristian system under which increasing millions are perishing in the finer aspirations and hopes of life? Tom's master was not to blame for the creation of the institution of slavery. It came before his day. But if his eyes had been opened—as yours, my friend, are to the evils of the present time—he could not have been blameless did he not raise his voice against it. He could have borne testimony, he could have protested in the name of a just God and an outraged humanity, and so can you today. Why sympathize with Tom and deny the claims of your white brother and his children in the next street?

My store in Jackson was on the main street and nearly opposite the capitol, a somewhat pretentious building, built of a yellowish native stone, "adorned" in front with massive "Grecian" columns, built of brick and plaster covered with a composition, supposed to imitate stone. It was surrounded by an iron fence, but the gates were always open and the grounds generally were not only open to the public but were somewhat ill-kept and wore an air of dilapidation. One day I noticed a small crowd of men standing about the capitol steps and on enquiring the occasion of the gathering was told that the sheriff was going to sell, on execution, a negro woman. I had never seen a sale of this character and hurried over and mingled with the crowd. Seated on the capitol steps was a rather small dark brown woman—pure blacks were the exception in all southern towns—apparently about thirty-five years of age. Her face was a study. Evidently she was rather more intelligent than the average "corn-field hand," but it was impossible to make out her feelings. Plainly, she had schooled herself in the matter of hiding her thoughts. Her face told nothing and was as impassive as that of a beast. She was not bad looking by anymeans and yet no gleam of the intelligence within shone upon her countenance. While still studying her looks a big strong armed negro man came through the gates, close by, bearing upon his head a dry goods box, brought from a store at hand. The box was placed upon the ground near the steps and the sheriff placing his hand upon the woman's shoulder, said: "Come girl, be lively now; look pleasant and may be you'll get a good master." His manner was not unkind and the "girl" rose and stepped upon the box; it was not more than two feet in height and the crowd, composed entirely of men and boys, gathered about it. "Gentlemen," said the sheriff, "I am about to offer at public sale the girl Ann, taken as the property of — — — to satisfy a judgment held by — — —. She is supposed to be about thirty years of age and is warranted free from disease or blemish. Now, gentlemen, how much am I bid?" The sheriff was here interrogated regarding the breeding qualities of the "property" offered for sale and replied: "O, she'll breed fast enough, only give her a chance." This caused a rude guffaw to go around, but the subject of the remark made no sign, her face was as impassive as ever. It was further elicited in this way that she had borne children, but nothing more. Nothing was said of them, of their age or where they were. The mother heard but she heeded not. In the usual attempt at talk made by the auctioneer he several times told her to "brighten up now a bit; show your ivories for the gentlemen," and the like, but she seemed not to hear and looked straight ahead. A man in the crowd asked to see her teeth and she opened her mouth disclosing a good set. Another with his cane poked her in the breast, "to see if there was anything there," he explained, and afterward with the same instrument partly lifted her dress to see what kind of legs she stood on. Other than this nothing very offensive was said or done. The crowd was not ill disposed; no harm was intended and the man who took the most liberties was only taking ordinary and proper precautions in the purchase of expensive property, for he intended to, and finally did buy her, at eight hundred and fifty dollars. This was the first time I had seen a human being put upon the auction block and the occurence made upon me a deep and lasting impression. Now, I can see that deprivation, come from what source and cause it may, necessitates degradation. Whoever deprives humanity degrades it as certainly as effect follows cause. Slavery deprived men and women and immediately degraded them to the level of brutes.

So today, by the cunning machinery of

rent, interest and profit the God given rights of millions of poor human souls are despoiled and destroyed. Done, too, by kindly hearted men and women who are ready to say: "Lord have we not in Thy name done many wonderful works?" Verily, they know not what they do.

Thomas Carlyle, that great English thinker, said of this in his country:

British and istrial existence seems fast becoming one vast prison—swamp of reeking pestilence physical and moral, a hideous Golgotha of souls and bodies buried alive.

Thirty thousand outcast needle women working themselves swiftly to death, and three million paupers rotting in forced idleness, helping the needle women to die.

From column after column of similar statements in our public prints the following is clipped from the New York Sun:

Dora Cavanaugh supports an invalid husband and two children in such comfort as there may be in three rooms in a dilapidated house, in a dilapidated row in a dilapidated part of West Nineteenth street at No. 144, by making vests. Carhart Whitford & Co., she said paid me 1½ cents for vests and it took me a whole day to do two and I had to pay for the button holes besides. Its worse than death to the young women that's what it is, sir she said. They try this sewing little and they soon see that there is no hope for them at honest work and they just go to the bad. I have seen it happen over and over again and a burning shame it is sir. Even if they stay at work they soon see what they must do if they expect any favor of the bosses.

Favor of the bosses! Think of it!! Will any man tell me that chattel slavery was immoral compared to the condition of affairs, here merely hinted at, and which we all know exists in appalling and constantly growing proportions? No, no, it was not, as God is my judge it was a far better system and much to be preferred.

And this from the St. Louis Chronicle. A newly made widow with four small children is speaking:

One day I wanted a bushel of coal but I only had 7 cents. Coal was 9 cents. The man said he would wait until I could pay the rest. Then my husband wanted a sour drink he had a burning fever poor fellow, and wanted a lemon so bad but I didn't have the two cents to buy the lemon—and I—and I couldn't get it. * * * * * * Oh, it seems as if I wouldn't have felt so bad when I saw his dear dead face in the coffin if I hadn't thought how he wanted that drink and and—I couldn't get it. I wake up in the night and think of it until it seems as if it will drive me wild."

The woman lived in a tenement and made pants at 85 cents a dozen!

The other day I received a letter from a kind old lady who said that when she read of the misery of the poor people in the cities that it made her feel wonderfully thankful to God who had placed her in so comfortable a position. She ought to have been ashamed to utter such a thought. Desire to seek out and save the poor victims of man's inhumanity should have swallowed up every other emotion. If God placed her in a comfortable position did he also place the poor girls of the cities in such an one as to insure their temptation, and their fall? What blasphemy!

The Robbery of Labor.

That deprivation does mean, and necessitate, degradation all careful observers are agreed. Well fed dogs are not apt to quarrel. But let them feel the pangs of hunger, then throw them together and the weakest soon will suffer. Gentlemen of wealth associate with mutual expressions of regard. Throw these same men together, in an open boat from foundered ship, and when the bread and water are gone wolfish eyes will be cast from one to another in the search for the easiest taken life. They then suffer deprivation. Degradation has begun. Take the best and most affectionate family you know; deprive them of their property; take from them the means of living honestly, decently and comfortably, confine them in a loathsome tenement house in some great city and when hope is gone they are ready for crime. Or, if, by chance, the elders "die and make no sign" their children will suffer in their stead—"even unto the third and fourth generation." And what of the almost countless thousands of the deprived and degraded children of poverty? Do not the "slums" bring forth thieves and prostitutes? And you knew it would be so. "Do men gather grapes of thorns, or figs of thistles?" But who are, and have been, responsible for the conditions which deprive? These are questions political, and politics in future must chiefly deal with the economic issue.

In the year 1860 I was engaged in keeping a store and running a postoffice at Terry's Station, sixteen miles south of Jackson, on the then newly built New Orleans, Jackson and Great Northern Railroad, now a part of the Illinois Central's Chicago and New Orleans line. The owner of the store and the holder of the commission was a practicing physician busily engaged in his profession. I was only a deputy p. m., but I did the work. Three lines of stages ran out from Terry's and all carried mail. Opposite the store stood the stage stable, belonging to Mr. Terry, who was also the mail contractor. Terry was a fat, jolly man about forty years of age, living upon his plantation about a mile away. He had a fine plantation, a most estimable family and about sixty negroes. His business of carrying mails and passengers gave him opportunity and excuse for a good deal of traveling about, which I am inclined to think he liked very much better than staying at home; not at all remarkable for most men with his opportunities would have done as he did. He often made trips to Cincinnati to buy horses and supplies and once a year, at least, went to Washington, so that he was pretty well informed regarding the North, Northern affairs and opinions. He had a pass on the railroad and made frequent trips to New Orleans. As he often went away and returned on trains passing Terry's during the night he had a room fitted up for his occupancy at the stable, and as I slept in the store it so happened that he was a frequent visitor at all hours of the day, and night. As I have stated he was a most companionable man, a great talker and also a particular friend of my uncle's, whose plantation lay some three miles away in another direction. It thus came about that he often freely and frankly gave me his opinions regarding slavery. I remember well his saying: "O, I suppose 'tis all right for I don't know what the negroes would do without masters to direct them, unless, as is quite probable, they fell back into barbarism. That's what took place in San Domingo. But it is all a great humbug for us; there is no pleasure in it, and what is worse there is no money in it, or but little. Fact is, it is not profitable to us, here on the hill lands. No one of us can make more than two per cent per annum on his capital. Some on the rich bottom lands may make more, but they are liable to overflow and to lose everything. Then, too, just think of it, I sleep with a revolver under my pillow and a double barreled shot gun right within reach at the head of my bed. And the women are always afraid of the niggers rising, so that they are frightened half out of their wits, if there happen to be a little more noise than usual at the 'quarters' of a night."

Mr. Terry told the truth straight as a string. For it a was fact that even with large capital it was almost impossible for men in his position, with cotton at 9 to 11 cents, the price then, to make both ends meet, if they happened upon a poor crop year or lost a "nigger" or two; their profits, where any were made, came from the monopoly of land, of which they held large areas. The small planters, the men with four or five negroes, who worked in the field with their slaves, and worked harder than they did—and there were many such—these, were the main stays and props of slavery. They all believed in it—religiously. Commonly they were men of little education, narrow in their views and full of prejudice. But the larger and wealthier planters had more leisure to read and think; generally they were men of education and most of them had been in the north or had traveled in Europe. Mr. Terry I found specially well informed and wonderfully frank in expressing himself. His experience in Ohio, where he had some friends or relatives, had opened his eyes. He knew perfectly well that he was farming his land and working his negroes "to get a profit out of the business," as he expressed it, or, as I can now see, stated more accurately, that he might obtain the fruits of labor. He took everything the negro had in the world and yet somehow the "business" was not as profitable as at the North. There, some friend of his had "invested" in land, was renting it out to a lot of poor white people, was furnishing them supplies from a store he kept, and charging interest on every advance, and at every crook and turn, and on much less capital he, the northern robber of labor, was beating the southern slave holder two to one.

In those days I knew nothing of economics, and I think Capt. Terry had made no special study of political or social economy, but he had "got right down to business" in his thinking, as I can now see, though I did not then. In short, Terry had discovered that in the robbery of labor the cunning modern machinery of rent, interest and profit is far more effective in depriving men, in robbing them, than was the outworn system of chattel slavery.

One day Terry came into the store saying: "I had quite an adventure a little while ago. As I was riding on horseback through the woods, I came upon two negro men that have been hiding out for a year past. They were in a little open place seated on the ground, cooking something. They looked up; I knew them both, one belongs to me, the other to B——.

"And what did you do?" said I, "did you speak to them?"

"Not I," said he, "I had no arms, and they are both big strong fellows and I know my man has a gun somewhere for he has been seen several times with it. The niggers all feed and harbor these 'layouters' and I suppose they have been having a regular picnic for a long time past."

"But didn't you try to capture the runaways?" said I.

"Well," said he, "I rode by them quite carelessly and as though I wasn't thinking much of them, and I so continued, until I got out of sight and then I put my horse down into a dead run for Andy C——'s. Andy and his dogs are after them now. I put them on the trail before I came in here."

The next day I was standing in front of the store when the cavalcade of man stealers came in; they stopped at the stable. Three or four men on horseback, a pack of eight or ten hounds and a stalwart man of color, with a rope around his neck and hand cuffs upon his wrists, made up the party. The end of the rope about the man's neck was fastened to the pommel of one of the saddles. Captured and bound the poor fellow's holiday was over. He was a fine specimen of physical manhood, strong and muscular. Dark brown in color he was what was then called a "griffe," that is, three quarters black. Hatless and shoeless he stood erect and with head thrown well back, a strip of what had been a shirt over one shoulder, one leg of his trousers completely gone, of the other a shred or two remained. Torn by the dogs, who stood whining and yelping by, his naked arms and legs were bleeding freely; but the spirit of the man was grand. He knew he had been brought to the stable to be whipped, but he stood erect and threw defiance at all around. He bitterly cursed and defied his captors in the most insulting and rebellious manner. They merely laughed and looked sheepishly at one another as he went on in the loudest and most excited manner.

to upbraid them. They had caught him for pay and were now to deliver him up, caring little what became of him. They could not beat him, it was Capt. Terry's nigger, and he had already been severely hurt, so they "stood it." I think this was the only time in all my life at the South in which white men were thus treated by a negro in my presence. I could but admire the man—and pity him. Capt. Terry was not at hand when the "boy" was brought in and he was taken into the stable and secured.

Terry did not whip him, or have it done, thinking, likely enough, that he had already been well punished.

Chattel slavery could treat men like this, could deprive them and degrade them, but it could not compare as a robbing machine with the modern smooth and insinuating methods. Now men are just beginning to wonder how it is that the holder of a mortgage can make more clear gain from a farm than the owner after he has added thereto his own labor and that of his poor tired wife and all his children. You see the devil hasn't lived all these years for nothing. He is getting "sharper" every day.

All wealth is created by labor applied to what are called "natural opportunities." That is, the soil, the mine, or the sea, etc., etc., and their natural products. In economic discussion these are usually grouped under the term, "land." It is impossible to conceive of the production of anything of value to man which is not thus created by the application of human exertion to land, or its natural products. Even the bread fruit must be obtained by labor. But ever since men have had an existence upon this round ball the supreme effort of most men, of the ambitious, the proud, the selfish and the covetous among them, has been to obtain wealth, or the fruits of labor, without themselves paying the penalty of toil. And this is the case today without diminution of desire, though veiled and hid

under craftier and more subtle methods, which to those under their spell appear legitimate and useful and capable of complete defence. But the devil is never dangerous save when he appears as an angel of light. Men talk of keeping the commandments! The first one is: "In the sweat of thy face shalt thou eat bread." Here reason, science and revelation agree. For whoever obtains anything from a fellow mortal without returning a full equivalent has robbed him to that extent. "We must all work or steal howsoe'er we name our stealing." If something less than a full equivalent is returned, a "profit" is said to have been made. But all profits are simply so much unpaid labor. Every man is entitled to the full value of all he has created. If you can not rightfully take all, as in chattel slavery, neither can you take a part, as in our modern thievery. But let me not be misunderstood. The merchant, who brings us coffee from Brazil, is entitled to reasonable pay for his service, but no more; if he obtains more, by artifice, by combination or by mere weight of money, as in the case of Arbuckle et al, he is a thief; no matter how many churches he bribes or preachers he pays, or colleges he endows, as in the cases of Rockafeller, Stanford and Gould. And the little thieves are just as much breakers of moral and ethical laws as the larger ones. True Christianity is forever opposed to all this, for the words of Jesus prove it, and our modern "Churchianity" is in as great need of a "reformation" as in the days of Luther, and every clear minded man with a grain of sense in his head knows it.

Rent, interest and profit, simply represent so much unpaid labor.

Lincoln's second message to congress contains the following. Was not Lincoln a prophet?

Monarchy itself is sometimes hinted at as a possible refuge from the power of the people In my present position I cou'd scarcely be justified were I to omit raising a warning voice against this approach of returning despotism It is not needed, nor fitting here that a general argument should be made in favor of public Institutions but there is one point with its connections, not so hackneyed as most others, to which I ask a brief attention. It is the effort to place capital on an equal footing, if not above labor, in the structure of the government. It is assumed that labor is available only in connection with capital, that nobody labors unless somebody else owning capital somehow by the use of it induces him to labor. * * * No men living are more worthy to be trusted than those who toil up from poverty; none less inclined to take or touch aught which they have not honestly earned Let them beware of surrendering a political power which they already possess and which if surrendered will surely be used to close the door of advancement against such as they and to fix new disabilities and burdens upon them until all of liberty shall be lost.

That so-called free labor is more profitable than slave labor all are now agreed. But many do not analyze this statement, do not really know what is conceded by it. If it is more profitable, then more profit is got from the labor. That is, more is obtained from him for which no equivalent is returned. Thinking himself free hope still beguiles him; he is more ambitious and produces more, and thus the modern manager is able to take vastly more from each "hand" than did the slave holder who took all. Half or two-thirds of a large sum may greatly exceed the whole of a small one. And it is found highly profitable by the modern "captains of industry" to foster in the minds of those upon whom they have fastened the burden of their support the idea of a personal freedom which in real truth does not exist. Men who pay tribute are not free. But men will delude themselves, even though the tribute they pay to a hundred concealed and smiling robbers exhausts all their means and powers of payment. All is gone, but in so many directions and to so many masters that they fancy they have none. Eyes have they, yet seeing they see not; ears have they, yet hearing they hear not, neither will they understand. And the greatest robber of all is Shylock, who, intrenched in law and

custom lies concealed behind, "good society," public institutions and the church, all of which if he be attacked immediately man their breastworks in his defence.

In the year 1862 British bankers, scenting the prey from afar, sent to this country one Hazzard, a London banker to teach our "financiers" how to coin gold from the blood of their countrymen, hoping incidentally to share in the spoil. He issued a confidental circular to "investors,' one paragraph of which is here printed. Our people were then new to this business and although widely circulated its full import was not at that time comprehended. Note carefully the ideas conveyed:

Slavery is likely to be abolished by the war power and chattel slavery destroyed. This, I and my European friends are in favor of, for slavery is but the owning of labor and carries with it the care of the laborer; while the European plan led on by England is capital control of labor by controlling wages. This can be done by controlling the money.

Thirty-two years ago was this published, and yet it is probable that a majority of our American voters cannot yet see that its every prediction has been fulfilled, and that the condition desired by "I and my European friends," to wit, the complete dependence of the producer upon the controllers of money, has been absolutely secured. "Wages" in this connection meaning not only the per diem of the laborer but also the pay or wages of the farmer and producer—for the price of the commodity produced is also completely controlled by the same means.

Ours is the "commercial age." "Formerly," says Carlyle," war was a business; now business is war." Formerly war and the plunder of a foreign nation were regarded as most commendable, and God was implored to bless and prosper it. Of course a convenient Deity was upon the side of "our" nation. Outside barbarians had no right to a God — they were not true believers. Then, they took all, and put the former owners to the sword. Now, we make "war" upon our neighbors, taking only a part of their substance. and plume ourselves upon our "honesty." Now, we slowly deprive our victims and lingeringly degrade them, congratulating ourselves, meanwhile upon the spread of "Christianity." Many methods we have, but the end sought is always the same—the robbery of labor. And God is asked to bless this, too.

About the year 1880 a large fortune, reputed at a million dollars, was left a young man, who at that time had just completed his studies in an eastern college. He was described as a young man of good habits and generous impulses who wished to leave the world at least a little better for his having lived in it. The fortune came to him unexpectedly and of course found him totally unprepared to undertake the weighty responsibilities incident to its management. Wishing to be of some service in the world he did not fancy the life of a drone living upon society without returning anything in the nature of an equivalent. Casting about in his mind as to the course he should pursue, his mind was drawn toward a plan of action involving the manufacture of a certain product. Thus, he thought, he would be enabled to help in the work of the world and incidentally to aid large numbers of people whom he might employ. But he was well aware that he possessed no particular knowledge of the business that had attracted his attention, nor had he the least business experience. Under these circumstances he knew perfectly well that he ran great risk of losing his capital if he engaged in business, and resolved to avail himself, so far as he should be able, of the advice and experience of the shrewd and hard-headed men of affairs. With this idea in his head he sought out among others a certain "Napoleon of the mart"—I think Phil Armour. Of this, however, I am not at this time positive, the newspaper slip giving the account having been mislaid. It was printed in a Chicago daily

and at the time attracted no attention, Armour's answer, upon which the interest of this anecdote hinges, being taken as a mere matter of "business," the attention of the general public not having at that time been directed to economic questions.

As a wealthy man and being armed with the necessary letters of introduction our young friend found no difficulty in approaching Mr. Armour and engaging him in conversation. Stating at length his business and his desire for advice Armour replied substantially as follows:

"Of course," he said, "you will understand that I can not give you special advice upon the particular line of manufacture to which you refer, having had no experience in that direction, nor can I give you special directions which will apply to your individual case. Every thing of that sort must be left to the time and the man. But there are a few general principles which I have found reliable and upon which, doubtless, you may also rely. You will need to employ a good many people; here, likely enough, will be found your greatest stumbling block, but if you keep one idea clearly in your mind you will be able to surmount all difficulties. It is this: You must employ no one who does not make you more money than you pay him. In short, your employes must make money for you. If you can manage that you will be able to accumulate money. For instance, suppose you engage in manufacturing. You must be shrewd in figures and know how to figure out the average value of a day's work. Get right down to business in this; find out what you depend on. If your hands are worth $1.50 to you, as a permanent proposition, you pay them 90 cents and you will be all right; that's the main point."

Now, there is not a particle of doubt in the mind of any business man that this was "good" advice; that is, advice tending to accumulate money in the hands of a master of men. And yet it advocated stealing from men and women who are placed by our system of slavery in such a deprived and dependent position that they can no more help themselves than could the negroes in chattel slavery. Invention and the power of money have destroyed the ability of the average laborer to employ himself. He is forced to seek a master; he becomes a mere machine, a cog in a wheel, which can at any time be replaced by idle "cogs" standing by, who gladly take the vacated place. And these idle men are a necessary part of the modern machine for the robbery of labor. For if only a part can find work, humility, cheapness and "thankfulness" on the part of the laborers are very much increased. They are easier managed. For if there are no unemployed the laborer soon becomes too independent for the master. He partially secures his freedom. But the great employers of labor are too "wise" to allow this. Their plan will not "work" without a reservoir of idle men. These are held as a club over the heads of men at work. Enmity between the two is encouraged. If union men fight 'scabs" the attention of both is taken from the sources of robbery. And as there must necessarily be large numbers of unemployed, in order that industrial thievery may have free course, men are daily deprived of the opportunity to toil and degraded into tramps. Not exactly "butchered to make a Roman holiday," but really degraded and beastialized, that our false and perjured "civilization" may live; that fashionable "dudes" may ruin the daughters of the poor and their fathers occupy the bald headed row at the ballet. Great Jove, where sleep thy thunders; and thy lightnings, will they never strike?

During my stay in the South I spent a month, one winter, in the city of New Orleans. I made the old Arcade hotel, on Poydras street, my stopping place. The Arcade took its name from its peculiar construction. It was built around an inner court after the oriental fashion. This inner court, or arcade, was roofed over with glass and made quite a spacious and satisfactory place for the hotel loungers and for the transaction of business. One end, or side, was sometimes occupied by slaves there exhibited for sale. One side had a long counter or bar with polite attendants behind it who sold fancy drinks and "red liquor." The slaves exposed for sale attracted from me a good deal of attention. In nearly every case they were arrayed in their best and whatever ornament each possessed was displayed with more or less taste and effect. I remember particularly a lot of about twenty-five or thirty, of all ages and sizes, and these were it then seemed to me, the healthiest, heartiest and most open-faced lot of slaves I had ever seen. They were all brown and light colored people, some of the girls being quite pretty. The man who had them in charge told me that they were the best lot of servants he had ever handled, being the entire lot belonging to a planter recently deceased and now, on this account, offered for sale. A very fine opportunity, he said, for obtaining servants that had been well raised by a man who took good care of them and brought them up right. He assured me that there was not a blemish on any one in the lot. After this I watched them with more interest than ever. I had, before this, read "Uncle Tom's Cabin"— t appeared in 1852—and could not help thinking of the sale of St. Clair's slaves after his tragic death, whenever I looked at them. I do not remember that I spoke to any of them but whenever a gentleman appeared who talked of buying, or examined the lot, if I happened to be near, I eagerly watched the demeanor of the captives and was quick to notice every look and tell tale glance of the eyes. Being told, probably, that it would be best for them to look pleasant and jolly the poor creatures did their best in this direction, but it was always a sorry effort. Having been raised together I presume they were mostly related, in one way or another, and so, of course, they we e extremely anxious rega·ding the disposition to be made of "the lot." Were they o be kept together or should they be separated? This was the constant ter- ro· before their eyes. And one could easily read it in their demeanor and in the replies made to questions asked them by prosp:ctive purchasers. They were treated with a good deal of c nsideration, and in the conversations bet⋈een would-be purchasers and the salesman he general y s id, we esire to sell such and such servants together, in fact, we prefer sell all together, or something of that sort. When anything of t is kind was said t was wonderfully interest ng t no e the appealing glances of the slaves. Their heart were in their eyes. O he dep bs of human misery! One day t ey failed to a·pe r and I saw them no more. What fate befei them I never knew.

I remember seeing h rd lo ing, dissipated me examining nd prici g the young women, not only at this time, bu at others B it t en men were forced to pay heavily for th s descripti of roperty. Now, youn white women, tenderly and affectionately reared, are obtaine I very much cheaper. Colored women, in those days had little idea of what we call virtue. They were never disgraced by what we call immorality, they were never bando ed, knew nothin of the shame of betrayal and in many instances, no doubt, their condition w s somewhat bett red b li·sons of this cha acter. I do not wish to be u derstood as saying one word in favor of immorality a: any time; I am now co paring on e il with another and a greater one. Then, young quadroons and ctaroons were kept in concubinage, a c ndition whic brough: them n shame or trouble, a condition which wa , an i s yet, countenance l y the Ol l Testament scriptures. The, slavery

carried with i care fo: the laborer—and the bond-woman. Now, our system debauches young white women and casts the n forth to suffer nd i . And our system is chiefly to blame in this matter. The chiefs of police of most of the gr at ities having united in a statement —published a few years ago—that the great and over shadowing cause of prostitution is the poverty of young women. It is caused by deprivation, nd deprivation is the necessary and absolutely certain result of a system built upon the robbery of labor, which we call "civi - zation;" and this system"good society," the church and most of t ose who call themselves respectable people, approve and defend. But the deprivation which is defended—the right to steal by law— is exactly and precisely the "rig t" claime by the slave ho der. In his day h was supported by the la v, by the church and all the preachers, in the South. and—they said—by the Bible. He who refused to belie e was an "infidel." An yet the legal right to a part of the labor of others, claimed by respectable people today who call themselves Christain is bitter y opposed by the Christianity of Jesus in every word and line of his teaching. And yet men who pretend to represent Him are found to defend the doings against which He launched the b tterest maledic ions. The scribes and phari:ees of His day appear again as the wealthy and sanctimonious worshipers of our time. "Whited sepulchers" they are and the " ead men's bon s and all uncle nness" with whic they are filled come from the robbery of "these little ones" whom the Go of Nature and of Justice will surely avenge.

Capital Versus Labor.

That eminent thinker John Ruskin says somewhere substantially: "Whereas, it has long been kn wn and approved that the poor have no r ght to the property of the rich; now, there fore, I desire it also to be known and admitted that the rich have no right to the earnings of the poor."

Ruskin here stated the marrow of the great question of the times, the question of capital vs. labor, with which the politics of the future must chiefly deal. Strenuous efforts have been, and will continue to be made, to conceal this from the minds of the public. But it will be labor lost, it cannot be longer done. For even the tariff discussion, with which it is sought to blind the eyes of men, is made to hinge upon the interests of capitalists upon the one side and the supposed benefits resulting to labor on the other. The time for deception upon this the main political question in this country has passed. But men who are perfectly well aware of this have not yet taken the places they will eventually occupy. Business interests, the hope of accumulating money, desire to "hold a job," society interests, and the like, prevent men everywhere from openly declaring what they know in tneir hearts to be true

A friend, not long since, engaged a squad of regular army soldiers, at Walla Walla, in conversation desiring to find out how they loked at political quest ons and was surprised to find them fully awake to the issues confronting the country. "We know perfectly well," said the soldier spokesman, "that the next great racket in this country will be between capital and labor, between the rich and t e poor, and we know, too, that the rich are counting on us to fight and kill po r men for them, but we are all poor men ourselves and they will find themselves mistaken. Of course, at first, when only a mob here and there opposes us we shall have to shoot as directed, but there won't be many killed in that way and when the real conflict comes on you will see how it will be." His comrades agreed with him, saying that this was the general feeling among the common soldiers, which they took extreme good care to keep from their officers.

This is given, not as indicating the feelings or opinion of the writer, for he regards all talk of an appeal to force in this matter as not only unwise and wrong in principle but also as tending to establish a military despotism in this country, but simply as a fact indicating the drift of public opinion. And public opinion in all modern countries is today the real ruling power. Sooner or later the government, even though this be a monarchy, must heed this power behind the throne. And it is curious to note that this general feeling that modern civilization, so called, is shortly to be tried as never before, has taken possession of thinking minds everywhere throughout the earth in direct opp sition to the urgent efforts of the great daily presses, the prominent pulpits and the constant teaching of tho e in official place and possessed of power and patronage. For all the e and many more, have hooted at the idea of the possibility of any conflict between cpital and labor, constantly itera'ing and reiterating the statement that the interests of the two are identical. But everybody capable of thought knows that this is not a c rrect statement, and th makers of it simply destroy their own credibility with the intelligent. That is all, 'or nobody believes it. Everybody knows that however it may be with capital and abor, taken abstractly and freed from human relations, that the pecuniary interests of t e capitalist and the abor r are as wide apart as the poles. The "interest" of the one is to obtain t e fruits of the laborer's labor without returning him a full equivalent, that is, to obtain somewhat which the laborer has created without paying him for it, or, practically, to hold him in slavery— to a certain extent. This same ' yarn" was constantly dinned into the negro's ears in the days of chattel slavery. He was told every day of the year that he ought to "dig in" and raise as much cotton for his master as possible, o that th master might be able to care for him better, to do more for his comfort, to give him more holidays, etc., etc. But although the preachers sang this song to the darkey every Sunday and his master filled in the rest of the week with the same story, he didn't believe a word of it. Now-a-days white men are found who believe in "protection" — to masters. But the negro knew better. He knew he would only get the usual two suits of cotton stuff, one wool hat, one pair of shoes in the winter, with the short Christmas holiday and the usual dole of corn meal and bacon. That was all he would get anyhow, and he knew it. The richer a planter got the harder his field hands fared. The negro saw that, and he was smart enough to "catch on." Northern white laborers may suffer in this comparison, but for that I am not to blame. Facts are stubborn things.

All students now admit Ricardo's "Iron law of wages;" which is: "Wages constantly tend to the lowest point at which the laborer will consent to labor and propagate his kind." "Wages," in this connection including, of course, the price of agricultural produce. The negro "consented" to labor and propagate his kind for the "wages" above enumerated. Of course that prevented white men from getting more for the same kind of labor. Resu t: the millions of "poor white trash," and the deprivation and consequent degradation of humanity. The Chinaman consents to labor for a series of years, without propagating his kind, at a very low rate, and wherever he comes in contact with white labor the result is the same as was the case with chattel slavery. Now, the pressure caused by combination among capitalist, competition among laborers induced by the increase of population, and the enormous weight of money and the constant greed of the capitalist seeking to obtain more and more of the fruits of labor, "for my money" induces men to consent to labor for so small a wage that they and their children are unable to avail themselves of the privileges

resulting from the enormous advances made by invention, machinery, science and art in the manners and customs of society. Capitalists, bo h large and small, unite in saying that these advances are not for the laborer; that he and his children and his children's children, must content them elves on the meagre possibilities of the past; that he and his kind must not think of these things, must give them up to the capitalist and be content to labor for him, even though it be known that all this advance, all this invention, all thi s machinery, and nearly all the science and art come from the toil both manual and mental, of men harrassed and weighted down by poverty. These are the fruits of labor—of hand or brain. The capitalist has create l none of these things, and yet he not only claims them but assumes "the right" to prevent other men from enjoying the fruits of their own labor, and proposes by means of the collection of rent, interest and profit to continually and forever absorb the fruits of labor.

He thus denies and rej cts the foundation stones of Christianity. The brotherhood of man he theoretically admits, but denies in practice. Doing unto others as he would have them do to him he utterly repudiates, for he says, practically, that the laborer must not consider himself in the same class with the capitalist. He creates two classes, in his mind, and denies the Christian obligation of the golden rule as existing between the two. This was exactly and precisely what the southern slaveholder did.

During my stay at the Arcade hotel, spoken of in the preceding chapter, I made the acquaintance of a nice old man of color who acted as waiter in the dining room. The hotel was run upon "the European plan," I think, and guests strolled into the refectory at any time that suited their convenience. There never was a crowd at any time and each was enabled to leisurely while away an hour if he chose. It so happened that it fell to the lot of the old man referred to to wait upon me; a small gratuity made him my friend and whenever I appeared he made every effort to serve me, standing very respectfully at the back of my chair while I was engaged at the table. A certain peculiarity in my diet made the old man think that possibly I might be a Virginian, and so one day after seeing that all my wants were supplied he said, speaking in a very low tone so that no one in the room might hear: "Young marster is you fum ole Virginny?"

"No, uncle, said I; what made you think so?"

"Wy," said he, you allus wants de cohn bread wiv you coffee, and dat de way dey did in Virginny, and I fought you might be fum dar, un mebbe you cum fum near de place whar I was bohn."

As the old man proceded in the most respectful and beseeching manner to relate his experience I became greatly interested. He told me that he had been sold away from Virginia more than thirty years before. He was a young man then He was parted from his wife and children, and though long years had passed never had he heard one word from them, nor had he met any one who could tell him anything of them, and so in the hope o hearing of them he had questioned me. Poor old m n. His heart was in his voice. Lonely, old, far from the scenes of his youth, he was without h pe r joy in life. He had been speaking to me from the back of my chair, but becoming intereste I in his pathetic story I turned partly around to look at him. His lip quivered and the tears chased one another down his cheek. What help was there for him? None, none; nothing could be done for him. Abandoned of man and bereft, as he

And yet this man's physical wants were well supplied, he was neatly dressed, he was a good waiter, his w rk was comparatively light and he was certain of a support through life and a decent burial at the close. What more, thought the master, could he ask?

Is the case not the same today with the capitalist and the laborer It is written that "man lives not by bread alone but by every word that proceedeth out of the mouth of God;" that is, the life of man comes rom those ennobling influences which proceed from the Spirit of Good. The pursuit of happiness is the occupation of all men and women. It is true that one seeks it in one way and another in another, but this is the business of every man's life, force I upon him by the constitution of his mind from which he cannot escape. That a man be a man it is absolutely necessary that he be able to hope in the future, for when hope is gone man is degraded into a devil. Some small gain in one direction or another must be his. The true interest of the laborer—as is the case with all—impels him to secure, if he can, an advance in the mental, social and material affairs of life; to make of himself the most possible. Every intelligent man, every religious man, knows perfectly well that the voice of God is heard, at some time during a man's life within his heart urging him to "come up higher"; he knows that this God-given desire is the foundation of all social and moral improvement among men, and he knows, too, that it will be impossible for the laborer to heed this call unless he is first able to make gain above his constantly recurring physical wants. The first step in mental advance is some degree at least of material comfort. Jesus fed the multitude first, afterward he preached to it. The capitalist, through the modern plan of combination among masters and competition among laborers, proposes by practical deprivation, in the manner fellows, from obtaining just and proper control over his own labor. Having done this he reduces the wages of labor, which by means of the advance of invention and the presence of the unemployed he is enabled to do, thus preventing the reasonable and proper aspirations of the laborer for himself and his children from ever being realized. The question at issue between the capitalist and the laborer is not only a p litical one but it is in a most eminent degree a moral and a religious one It is the question of the ages; the devilish power of greed against the rising claims of humanity; an irrepressible conflict, upon which wait the hopes and aspirations of men; for until it is settled, and settled as it should be, moral development in the world is at an end. The multitude must first be fed. But the capitalist will claim to the end that he has "a right " to some portion of the laborer's product, for if he could not possess himself of it he himself would be obliged to labor, and to this he is opposed.

But for the laborer no hope appears—while he remains a laborer. The capitalist, and the apologists for capitalism, tell him that They say: "Work, save, collect interest from some other laborer. Get some form of legal advantage over men poorer and more dependent than yourself; do as we have done, do anything to get out o' the position of a laborer; then you may hope, but not otherwise."

And this too, was often told the negro. Trusty negroes, in the towns, were often allowed to hire their own time, and if by hook or crook they were able to earn more it was their own. Some, in this way bought themselves, but many tried to do this where few succeeded, Now, the pressure of capitalism upon white labor is already so great that the opportunity of the white to free himself is little better, if any, than was that of the black bondman in the past.

hope, are looking to the future with fear and dread. Despair is taking hold upon the masses as never before in this country. They see that if things are to remain as they are that they have no hope in the world. To assist, to uphold, to encourage men, to help, in some small measure, at least, in removing the evils of the time is surely the noblest work which can engage the human mind. And yet if a man engage in an inquiry into the causes of the monumental injustice of the present, and make known the result, immediately most receivers of the stolen goods of the laborer spew upon him their envenomed slime.

Jesus, the first great labor reformer, said: "Ye cannot serve God and mammon." But most of those who profess to follow him are, practically and in fact, engaged in an attempt to prove him a liar.

The Labor Question.

Thus far the argument stated in these chapters is to the effect that wealth, the power of money, or mammonism, which is the controlling force of the present day and time, is engaged in the effort and attempt to secure power over labor by deprivation, which necessarily results in the degradation of humanity. Many, no doubt, who have followed thus far will refuse to assent to this rather plain statement of the case. They will say that it is not the desire, or intent, of the accumulators of money to decrease the opportunities, enjoyed by the common herd. But that this is the result and the absolutely necessary and certain result, of all their actions admits of no dispute. For if we look carefully at the matter we see that the power of money depends entirely for its force upon the absence of money in the pocket of him it is desired to influence. If all were possessed of an abundance none would be found to perform menial service. The necessities of the poor form money may have power, it is essential that some be without it and desire it. If we suppose a condition of society in which every member thereof is possessed of houses and lands, flocks and herds and all the attributes and belongings of a vast estate, we shall at once see that power of one man over another is absent. It no longer exists. If the holder of all this wealth desires work to be done he must himself perform the labor; for those to whom he might apply would also desire him to labor for them. If each possessed, under these circumstances, an equal amount of gold it would then be discovered that its purchasing power had largely disappeared.

The final results of an equality of riches is to force all to labor in some useful capacity. Rather than starve the holder of the vast estate we have spoken of would plough his own field and dig his own garden. But if we suppose, still farther, some great convulsion of nature by means of which large numbers of these same wealthy landed proprietors lose their possessions and are reduced to poverty, they are then forced to apply to those who have not so lost their wealth for employment. Immediately, wealth in the hands of the few, which when possessed by all had lost its force, regains its power. It has now power over labor. Before it had not. And its power in this instance, as in all others, depends upon the necessities and the poverty of the many. Without this poverty, without these necessitief, it would lose its power to oppress. Hence the prevailing desire on the part of mammonism, capitalism, the money power, or whatever name be used to express the prevailing power of wealth, to deprive others of wealth, to deprive others of the good things of life. (For the illustration of the estates I am indebted to that eminent thinker John Ruskin and I am glad in this connection to commend to all lovers of truth the works of to great a man.)

Still, in spite of all that has been, or can be said, it is probable that most of my capitalistic readers will refuse to believe themselves engaged in the work of depriving and degrading their brothers and sisters of the human family, or, if compelled to see that this is the certain result of their actions and their lives, they will, it is likely, shield themselves, in their own minds, behind the laws and permissions of society. But for these laws and permissions it still remains that each is personally responsible. Whoever assists in upholding these laws and these conditions is responsible, so far as his individuality is concerned, for the known and certain results. Many a high born and well bred lady dares not think of the horrors of the slaughter house. In fact, most people look with horror upon the brutalities there enacted, and yet but for the patronage of the wealthy and the cultivated and the generous by far the larger share of this carnage wou'd cease. Wealth pays for "the best cuts." It makes the business profitable. It furnishes the incentive. The high born dame, during the course of her life, destroys many lives. Her riot causes the lamb to bleed and die. In like manner the demands of her sensitive and perverted nature, in many ways, which it is not necessary here to specify, cause the deprivation, the degradation, the sorrow and the misery of many members of the human family. Indeed she will not be content unless they are deprived. They must not aspire to equal "their betters." Now these conditions, this deprivation, this degradation, this vast misery into which humanity in the mass is plunged are the plain and certain results of the laws and regulations of society. These laws and regulations are made and enforced or repealed and modified by political combinations, and in no other way. Hence the consideration of all efforts to permamently improve the condition of society is the legitimately subject and object of politcal combination. This is poitics—"the science of government."

Once upon a time during the earlier part of my life at the South I received an invitation from the young ladies of a certain family to attend a merry-making at their house. I was told that the occasion was the marriage of a young quadroon house servant, the favorite waiting maid of one of the white ladies. On account of the fact that she was a favorite her marriage was to take place in "ole misstis" best room and was to be preceeded by a general jolification, eating of sweet meats, ice cream, and the like by the "white folks," the house servants and a few invited guests, both white and colored. The invited colored people coming only from the specially favored ranks of the house servants of the near vicinity. I suppose I can say that upon this occasion I was a favored guest. I went early and in company with the young white ladies of the house watched with great interest the peculiar actions of the colored people. For the time they were the honored guests. The occasion was theirs. And it was just such a time as the apologists for slavery would have chosen to present the beauties of "the peculiar institution." Although the white people kept a little to themselves there was a constant mingling of white and black in the festivities. All the slaves were quite tastefully dressed in the scarcely worn cast-off finery of their masters and mistresses and the greatest good nature prevailed. Indeed, it used to be said in Jackson that on Sunday the black people out-dressed the whites, and if bright colors be taken into the account I presume this was true. I remember that I carried there from Boston a pair of, then, fashionable $12 pants, very large plaid, black and dark green. Our older people will remember that a short time previous to the late war large plaids and fancy colors were "the proper thing." It was even said that plaids so large were used that two men must stand side by side to show the pattern. In those days of slower communication fashions also were somewhat slow in making their way to the West and South. So, it happened that when I arrived in Jackson with those black and green plaids they just took the eye—of the niggers. "Boys will be boys," you know. However, I hadn't been in the Southern capital a week before I had at least a dozen applications for "dose pants, wen you gets done wiv em." I can't remember what I did with them but I don't think I kept them long. They were too conspicuous there.

But to the marriage: After an hour or two of innocent rollicking fun the bride and groom "stood up" in the best room, the white folks were given seats of honor upon one side and the colored people crowded the other sides and every door and window with smiling and expectant faces. I then, for the first time, bethought me of the preacher and asked one of the ladies of the house who was to officiate. "Oh," she said, "Jim can do that; this is a negro wedding you know." I had not been long in the South at the time and was immensely taken back, for Jim was a slave and the plantation clown and maker of jokes and songs. I was amazed that the ladies of the house, ladies of the highest "quality," church members and perfect patterns of propriety in all matters relating to white society should thus make a mock of the marriage relation. But they did, all the same. Jim was called in and went through a rigmarole intended only to "make fun." The ne_ groes laughed but I could see little to amuse in his gyrations. After the "marriage" the negroes adjourned to "the quarters" and, it was said, danced all night.

These ladies assisted in the degradation of their sisters and their sex without, I suppose, the slightest compunction of conscience, and so do ladies today as clearly and as openly as then.

Then, one of the constantly iterated and reiterated "advantages" of slavery was stated to be, what was probably the fact, that it saved the white women from "immorality." Colored women were degraded, therefore, white women were "saved," therefore, the degradation of colored women was a good thing. This was the argument. Unchristian, immoral and ridiculous one might truthfully say and yet it is the sole and only argument advanced to-day in support of what we euphoniously call our "civilization." Freedom from toil and leisure to think are said to be the first steps toward a higher development, therefore, some must labor more, that others be "saved" from toil. This is the argument, get it from whom you will, whether it be the chancellor of a university or an ignorant millionaire. They know perfectly well that the imperative command of nature, addressed to all mankind, to labor—"In the sweat of thy face shalt thou eat bread"—is mandatory upon all and that no man ever did or ever will escape it without, in some way, throwing upon others the burden of his support. Thus, the effort of life being to secure advantage over our fellows, success in this felonious attempt is possible without our own increase, provided others be deprived. If it be made twice as difficult for others to obtain our dollars the value of our money has been doubled. That this is the effort of men all careful students are forced to admit, for conceal it as we may from others—and from ourselves—the end and aim of all "riches" is power over men, power to control them for our advantage. At bottom this is what is sought, and this object is more readily gained by the decrease of the opportunities of others than by the increase of our own. Hence this is the direction generally taken by men who would be rich. As an instance take the recent attempt to destroy organized labor. One would think that as his labor was the sole capital of the poor man that he ought to be able to combine in order to control it; but no, this will not be allowed and the courts are set in motion to deprive, in order that humanity may be degraded and the relative position and power of the capitalist be enlarged and increased.

It has been well said that one may be placed so near to a cathedral that he is not able to behold it. His eyes see only a block of stone. So today we are so close to the labor question that without divesting our minds of the powerful claims of self-interest it is impossible for many to behold the immense importance of this question and its answer, that greatest socialistic utterance ever promulgated, "Do unto others as ye would that they should do unto you," for if this were put into practice an end would be made to the chief and principal endeavor of mammonism, now the ruling religion of the day, to deprive and degrade humanity.

Organized labor, too, has its motto: "An injury to one is the concern of all." In sentiment, intent, and meaning it is identical with the saying of Jesus, and yet witness the bitterness with which His professed followers in the ranks of capitalism, or mammonism, assail the men who hold to it, as "anarchists" and socialists; for so ignorant are they that in their eyes one term is as applicable and as opprobrious as the other. Scarcely less bitter is the opposition of the mammonists to the motto of the People's party, "Equal rights to all and special privileges to none"—substantially the same in meaning. For, instinctively, though ignorantly, it is recognized that somebody, some men, some class, must be deprived and degraded that the importance and illicit gains of mammonism be not decreased.

And this deprivation is the immediate cause and parent of most of the evil now crying for remedy in the world. In England it has been proved by carefully collected statistics that crime steadily increases with the price of bread. Students of penology all know that poverty is the greatest single cause of crime. Deprive a boy at home of innocent enjoyment and if given an opportunity he "paints the town red." Deprive a girl in like manner and you have taken the first steps in the manufacture of a harlot. The horrors of the French revolution came as the necessary result of the awful subjection and deprivation of "the third estate" endured for years in silence. Human nature is like the pendulum; if swung to one side it will rush toward the other.

The other day a friend told me the sad history of a young girl in Seattle. Her father was a farmer, forced by the hardness of the times to deny his family. Hard work, long hours and poor fare tell the story. Debt and the payment of interest money swallowed all. Home under these circumstances had little charm for her. Her parents were not unkind but the necessities of their situation were so exacting that little room was left for sentiment or a display of affection.

But knowledge to their eyes her ample page
  Rich with the spoils of time did ne'er unroll.
Chill penury repressed their noble rage
And froze the genial current of the soul.

To Seattle she came, hoping for that "chance in life," that ability to pursue happiness which is the birthright of every child of humanity. Great God why is it denied to any? Half starved mentally and supplied by nature with that fatal embellishment, beauty, small space of time had passed until she met a man who seemed to her immature and unfurnished mind the personification of every noble quality. He promised everything, loaded her with presents and awoke within her heart the divine passion. Her life should no longer be the dull and cheerless thing it had been. New visions came and hope, that daystar of the heart, arose and flooded all with mellow light.

Alas, poor child, the usual result followed, the usual wreck, the usual ruin, the usual despair. Society will vent its impotent spleen upon the poor victim. Already the principal sufferer, it will add its heartless reproaches to her sorrow. Churchianity will speak of the guilt of the seducer—and receive him with open arms to its levees. The evolutionist will sigh, tell us of the survival of the fittest, but offer no hope, no solution. For us it is left to declare that the creators of the conditions surrounding humanity, the High Priests of Mammon, ae chiefly to blame. Comrades let us pursue them to the end. Their methods shall be exposed.

The Rights of Man.

The competitive system, or the war of business, is slowly dying. The trusts have shown us the way of deliverance. Combination and mutual agreement will finally take the place of the present predatory warfare. But in place of the present syndicates and combines controlling the vital energies of the nation, and sapping its life, must stand the whole body of the people. Then peace and contentment will prevail and the pursuit of rational happiness be possible to all. A new order, a new age, a new world, will have been born and the Christ that is yet to reign in the hearts of men will become a present reality. Back, then, to the owls and bats with the night of the wretched past, the age of competition and hate and war. All hail! the coming day of peace on earth and good will to man! Speed the time of deliverance and of hope! Help! for the hard-pressed and the sorrowing. "These little ones" demand our aid. For in this work of assistance he who hesitates is lost and he who doubts is damned.

Behold this was the iniquity of thy sister Sodom: pride, fulness of bread and prosperous ease was in her and in her daughter: neither did she strengthen the hands of the poor and needy.—Ezekiel 16:49.

Let us once more very briefly examine the foundations upon which we as human beings stand in this world of ours.

First, then, all men have from nature, or from God, certain inherent, or natural, rights. These make, in part, at least, the nature of man; they are inseparable from him. To circumscribe or deny them, in whole or in part, destroys wholly or partially the man. And while they are circumscribed or denied peace is impossible and justice an idle word. The American Magna Charta clearly sets forth these facts:

We hold these truths to be self-evident that all men are created equal; that they are endowed by their Creator with certain inalienable rights that among these are life, liberty and the pursuit of happiness That to secure these rights governments are instituted among men.

Jefferson and the Continental Congress thus built upon the only true foundation, the inherent and imprescriptible rights of humanity. Whatever interferes or contravenes is wrong, and not only wrong but void, and hence not binding upon the moral sense of society, constitued as it should be. For, surely, no argument is needed to prove that if men are denied natural, that is, God given, rights that or 'er, security and general happiness, to make no mention of justice, are impossible among intelligent and self-respecting people. To further fortify this important position, this foundation of right among men, to wit: That man's authority for existence and his claim to happiness rests upon Nature and natural law—the hand of God, as seen by man—and that the denial by men of these laws of God is the origin of all political disturbance, let us refer to that grand declaration of the rights of men and of citizens, issued by the National Assembly of France in 1789:

The representatives of the people of France, formed into a National Assembly, considering that ignorance neglect or contempt of human rights are the sole causes of public misfortunes and corruptions of government, have resolved to set forth in a solemn declaration those natural imprescriptible and inalienable rights, and do recognize and declare, in the presence of the Supreme Being and with the hope of His blessing and favor the following sacred rights of men and of citizens:"

1—Men are born and always continue free and equal in respect of their rights. Civil distinctions therefore, can only be founded upon public utility.

11—The end of all political associations is the preservation of the natural and imprescriptible rights of liberty, property, security and resistance of oppression.

Jefferson tells us, in the Declaration, that governments are instituted to secure these natural rights. Practically, and truthfully, he says that unless these rights are secured, to the weakest and the humblest, that governments have no moral right to exist.

Of these statements of Jefferson that greatest American, Abraham Lincoln, wrote the following whole-hearted and grand endorsement:

SPRINGFIELD, ILLINOIS, April 6, 1859,
To Messrs. Henry L. Pierce, and others.

GENTLEMEN—Your kind note inviting me to attend a festival in Boston on the 13th instant, in honor of the birthday of Thomas Jefferson was duly received. My engagements are such that I cannot attend.

*   *   *   *   *

It is now no childs play to save the principles of Jefferson from total overthrow in this nation. One would state with great confidence that he could convince any sane child that the simpler propositions of Euclid are true; but, nevertheless, he would fail with one who should deny the definitions and axioms. The principles of Jefferson are the definitions of free society. And yet they are denied or evaded with no small show of success. One dashingly calls them glittering generalities; another styles them self-evident lies, and another insidiously argues that they apply only to superior races. These expressions differing in form are identical in object and effect—the supplanting the principles of free government—and restoring those of classification, caste and legitimacy. They would delight a convocation of crowned heads plotting against the people. They are the vanguards, the sappers and miners of returning despotism. We must repulse them, or they will subjugate us. This is a world of compensations and he who would be no slave must consent to have no slave. Those who deny freedom to others, deserve it not for themselves, and under a just God they cannot long retain it.

All honor to Jefferson—to the man who in the concrete pressure of a struggle for national independence by a single people, had the coolness, forecast and capacity to introduce into a merely revolutionary document an abstract truth applicable to all men and all times, and so embalm it there that to day and in all coming days it shall be a stumbling block to the harbingers of reappearing tyranny and oppression. Your obedient servant,   A. LINCOLN.

But what are these "inalienable rights?" We are told that "among these are life, liberty and the pursuit of happiness," They are not fully and explicitly stated. For, it must be manifest to all, it was impracticable to include in what Lincoln calls "a merely revolutionary document" a full statement embracing the rights of men upon this earth. But this is plain: If men have certain natural rights they are also by nature's law fully entitled to whatever is given by nature essential to the preservation of those rights. If men receive from God the right to life they also have from Him the full title and patent to such natural opportunities—provisions of nature—as are essential to that life while it lasts. Air is essential to life. To deny it is to destroy life. If men are entitled to liberty, whatever nature—or God—has given to the race necessary and essential to liberty is also included in the grant. If the right to pursue happiness is inherent in man; if it is a gift of the Creator, then whatever the Creator has provided for all mankind which is essential to that pursuit belongs also to every child born into the world, by right divine. All this needs no proof. For, every man knows that the right to life is denied if air be withheld. And so of other essentials not here specified. But these essentials are not in anywise the creation of man. Hence, men can not rightfully claim to "own" them. "All men," said Jefferson, "are endowed by their Creator" with these rights. They came by the fiat of God from the womb of Nature, the common mother of us all. Wealth belongs to him who creates it; but natural opportunities were not created by man and hence can never rightfully be the sole and separate property of man. The right to use only is given.

Thirteen years after the issuance of our Declaration the wise men of France not only restated the rights of men as "liberty, security, property and resistance of oppression," but they also, still further, stated the self-evident fact, "that ignorance, neglect or contempt of human rights are the sole causes of public misfortunes and corruptions of government." No student will deny this. The pages of history are full of corroboration. In fact, it is the one lesson of the past to which there is no exception. The downfall of a nation has invaribly been preceded by the exactions and impositions of a favored class. The natural rights of men were ignored, neglected or condemned. Then came the end. And the end was the natural and righteous judgment of God against those who thus broke the laws of nature; and in this both human and divine nature are included, for both are equally the will of God.

Blackstone tells us in his principles of law that all statute laws in contravention of divine or natural law are void. He also tells us that all valid law is based upon that natural and instinctive apprehension of justice which finds universal lodgement in the heart of man. To this let us turn. If we suppose a company of people to be wrecked and cast upon a hitherto undiscovered island in the midst of the sea we shall shortly arrive in our minds at an understanding of the rights which each one of this company would have upon the island. And, first, this would appear to be a right not only to life but also to whatever existed upon the island necessary to its preservation. Each has a right to apply his labor to existing natural opportunities. He would have a right to fish in the sea, to cultivate the soil for the support of himself and those dependent upon him and to use whatever coal, stone or timber the island afforded absolutely necessary to warm and shelter them. To this extent his title or natural right would be ample. To all these things no one could have a greater right than any other. And these rights exist only when exercised. No man could then say, as Henry George has said, that he did not wish to apply his labor to land but the time would never arrive when he should cease to demand his share of the proceeds of the labor of others when applied to land.

Should one undertake to do this he would then appear in his true light as a monopolist, pure and simple, and the people of the island would make short work of his pretensions.

So far there would be, there could be, no quarrel among the colonists. Each family or company among them would proceed to the erection of such houses, cabins or other shelters as they might be able or willing to construct. Later, clearings would be made and if possessed of seeds and plants, cultivation of the soil would be begun. Certain locations would be agreed upon as the working places or fields of each worker. The right, in this way, to use the soil would be immediately and universally conceded as based upon the "natural and instinctive apprehension of justice." But no claims to individual ownership would be set up for all would recognize the fact that their stay upon the island, until rescued, might be very short. Nothing, however, would hinder the people from "swapping," trading or, indeed, giving up altogether locations previously assigned and "improved" or labo-ed upon. Some one of the company may have built a boat and established a fishery, exchanging with the land workers the products of toil, and for this boat one might sell his "claim." The exchange would be equitable, but for his boat the owner would only receive "a claim," not the land itself and he could only hold it by living and laboring upon it. Otherwise his title, which comes from his necessities, lapses. One could scarcely claim pay for the excess of air which the laborer uses because of his labor. So, he who refuses to apply his labor to land is barred from demanding from the agricultural labor any portion of his produce. "He that will not work neither shall he eat."

As time passes, if the people of the island are not rescued, they gradually improve their condition by the erection of more commodious houses, by increasing the size of their fields and the amount and number of their products. After a time, having settled, or built houses and cleared fields, in various parts of the island engaged in the production of various crops and products, exchange of products, or trade, gradually comes to occupy a constantly increasing importance. This calls for the building of roads and the erection of bridges, some primitive form of money, or evidence of debt, and finally, perhaps, the establishment of a system by means of which information or messages may be conveyed from one part of the island to another. Now when all these are established and in full operation, if each is free and secure in the possession of what he has created, it will appear, I think, that the inhabitants of t e island are in full possession of their natural rights. The statement of these natural rights may be still further simplified by saying that these consist in the right to life, liberty and security in the possession of property, the right to apply labor to natural opportnities for self support, and the right to exchange freely the products of labor, whether of hand or brain, subject in each instance to the equal rights of others. These are natural rights, all others are artificial and conventional. In the settlement of the rival claims of labor and capital it is imperative that these natural rights be preserved and maintained unimpaired to all, both high and low, rich and poor, great and small. For nothing can be a settlement, nothing can be right, which denies or circumscribes these natural, or God given, rights of man upon the earth.

What "the natural and instinctive apprehension of justice" would dictate in this direction, if given opportunity, forms the subject of the next chapter.

The Beginning of Evil.

If we suppose time to pass and the population of our island to increase, it will probably be found that events proceed much after the following fashion: After a time the inhabitants become measurably satisfied with their condition, and most of those born upon the island regard it as much the best place to live in all the world, discounting, in their minds, the stories of the elders in regard to other lands: And even these, having finally and with much labor subdued the wilderness, cultivated fields, built houses and established industries, cannot bring themselves to leave the property thus created when given an opportunity to do so by the arrival of ships and the establishment of communication with the rest of the world. Quite early in the history of the island it might be discovered by one of the company that a certain shallow pool near the shore—the only one of the kind upon the island—filled with sea water at high tide through a narrow inlet, might be readily and easily dammed at the inlet so as to prevent the escape of the water. The rays of the sun, he reasons, will be sufficient to evaporate the water, leaving a deposit of salt, which being removed and the dam opened for the admission of more water, a salt manufactory is established. Accordingly he "takes his claim" along side the pool, dams the inlet and shortly has salt to exchange. As this is the product of his own labor no fault is found at first to the arrangement, and his title to all the salt upon the island is gradually and in process of time perfected. Shortly he himself is not obliged to labor, and by raising the price of salt he slowly begins to accumulate the results of other men's labor; for in order to obtain this necessity men must give up some portion of time and effort. Hiring other men to do the work he lives in ease, being able to appropriate the labor of others, After his death his descendents occupy in his stead. With them title has become absolute. Their right to the natural opportunities embraced in he "salt works" is, they suppose, un-

questionable. The price of salt is now high, and the ability of the "proprietors" to take from the islanders the fruits of labor is almost unlimited.

If any objection is made the objecton is told that he is a disturber of the rights of private property; that the accumulation of property is the incentive to progress and improvement; that without it men would speedily lapse into savagery and degradation. Civilization, they will tell him, like everything else of value, costs something. So, in order to secure the benefits and blessings of civilization something must be paid. The theory advanced being that on entering upon the establishment of government each citizen gives up certain rights for the benefit of society. This is the price he pays—the cession to the community of a portion of his natural right. This is the theory upon which government is now based, but it is the convenient hook upon which is hung wrong, injustice and deprivation, with its attendant degradation. The results are before us in the world. Progress is attended by poverty; and the greater the progress of the few deeper and more bitter becomes the poverty of the many. The larger the city and the greater its advantages, to the few, the more hideous the degredation of the many.

But that the theory, the principle upon which this deprivation of the masses is based, is false ought to be clear to every well endowed mind. For among all the millions of men none can be found who have knowingly agreed to the cession of any portion of their own individual rights. The thing is false. And it is seen, too, in modern society, constituted as it now is, that the cessions made, as in the case of the salt manufacturer, though nominally to the community and for the benefit of society at large, are really made to individuals and corporations. They receive all the benefit. Society gets none. Indeed, in this way society, or the general public is made to compass its own destruction for the benefit of the few. Everybody who buys salt on the island gives up the fruits of his labor to him who labors not. He thus increases the wealth and power of the monopolist by adding to his own poverty. And all at the command of that misinformed, uneducated and unchristian sentiment which deprives men and calls the machinery of deprivation "civilization." But this is a misnomer. The word civilization comes from civis, a citizen; the word civil from the same root, plainly co.veying the idea of regard for the rights of others, or altruism.

'Our manners, our civilization, and all the good things connected with manners, and with civilization, have in this European world of ours depended for ages upon two principles—the spirit of a gentleman and the spirit of religion.' —Edmund Burke.

Burke here tells us what civilization properly is—what it should be. Plainly what we now have is not that. The spirit of a gentleman and the spirit of religion are absent. What now passes under the name is simply the rule of the stronger—in these days, the richer—civilization it is not.

The real truth is that the "saltworks," being a natural opportunity, a gift of the Creator and not the result of any man's labor, belong to the whole people of the island, who should take possession of it, remunerating the "owner" for all his expenditures, and operate it for the good of all, disposing of the salt at the cost of production. This would be true civilization applied in this case. And nothing short of this treatment will fit the case, for no other plan will preserve to the individuals comprising this society their natural rights. That would settle the salt question for the islanders. And it is in entire conformity with Blackstone's dicta that all valid law derives its final authority from that natural and instinctive apprehension of justice having a lodgment in the hearts of men, and that statute law overriding or contravening natural law is void. The

condition of the islanders subjected to the impositions of a salt monopoly is abhorrent to this natural and instinctive apprehension, and the laws, rules or regulations by means of which it maintains its authority are clearly and plainly, in this instance in contravention of natural law. Hence, in real truth, they are void.

If we follow the probable course of events among the islanders we shall see that monopolies gain their power and exert their swa. by depriving the people, under various alluring and deceptive pretexts of their natural rights. The claim would then be set up, as it is to-day, that this is necessary to the general good. But the claim is always made by the interested few, and is intended solely for their benefit. The natural rights of men upon the earth are few in number but it is impossible that a true civilization, conveying the greatest good to the greatest number, can exist unless these are fully conceded and accorded. It is not necessary, it is not just, it is not in accordance with the precepts of Christianity nor is it wise, that the natural right of any citizen, bounded as it is by the equal right of every other citizen, should be in the slightest degree denied or abridged, for here is the beginning of evil.

Probably the most important natural right of man upon the earth is the right to that life which has bee thrust upon him by the Creator. This carries with it the right to a foothold upon the earth. The world in which we live is the gift of God to the race, to humanity, not to a favored few. All our paper titles run back to some robbery, some bold assumption of right proceeding from might. The weak have ever been dispossessed and disinherited. The natural, or God-given right of man has been denied. The Hebrew scriptures are full of passages showing that the right of the "owner" of land is only that of occupation and use. Read the following with the contet:

"The land shall not be sold forever, for the land is mine; for ye are stangers and sojourners with me.

And in all the land of your possession ye shall grant a redemption for the land."'Lev. xx. 23—24.

Blackstone thus sums up the legal and religious view of the matter:

In the beginning of the world, we are told by Holy Writ, the all-bountiful Creator gave to man dominion over all the earth and over the fish of the sea and over the fowls of the air and over every living thing that moveth upon the earth." This is the only true and solid foundation for man's domain over external things, whatever airy, metaphysical notions may have been started by fanciful writers upon the subject. The earth therefore and all things therein are the general property of all mankind, exclusive of all other beings, from the immediate gift of the Creator." -Blackstone's Commentaries, II 2.

The national Free Soil convention of 1852, really the first Republican convention, has this to say:

"All men have a natural right to a portion of the soil, and as the soil is indispensible to life, the right of all men to the soil is as sacred ss the right to life itself."

But men have been usually "civilized" out of these footholds upon the earth by the machinations of the money changers. Anciently men lost their lands precisely as they are losing them today; they pledged them to the usurer. Read the fifth chapter of Nehemiah for a full description of the methods in use today, also for proof of the fact that one per cent per annum, or the hundredth part, is usury—or use money—the meaning of the word as used by Shakspeare, Bacon and the translators of the Bible.

Let us suppose that upon the arrival of the shipwrecked people at the island it is found that one has been able to bring to land his bag of gold and silver coins. The other passengers, in the hurry and confusion of shipwreck thought little of money. Not so with one, who braving all in his attachment to gold brought his coin safely to shore. At first little was thought of this. All the energies of each were at once devoted to the task of self-preservation, that first impulse ef nature. Shelters

were to be built, and a place of safety to be provided for the provisions saved from the wreck. In this all perforce took part. No one could hire another to perform his part of the work, for the labor of all was imperatively demanded. Indeed, some time elapsed before any could be spared from the labor required for the commonweal. After a time, however, that portion of the cargo which drifted ashore having been duly housed and protected and cabins more or less comfortable provided for all, the settlers began to look about them and take thought for the future.

As the hope of immediate rescue gradually faded away it was seen that as the provisions left could not last forever something must be done to provide more for the future. So, each one began to say: "There is fertile land, we have seeds and plants, why then should we not proceed to plant and cultivate?" And this, after much discussion, it was decided to undertake. As in all companies of men and women some are active and energetic and others slothful and dilatory, so among our settlers these varying qualities had place. Thinking this over the wise among them strongly advocated the plan of separate action in the every day work and duties of life, agreeing to combine in all matters concerning the general and public welfare. In this way, it was argued, each one would be free to manage his private concerns in such way and manner as should be pleasing to him, thus securing that freedom and harmony without which it would be impossible to live quiet and peaceable lives. It thus came about that without inharmony or strife it was agreed that each should select "a claim" and devote himself to the work of home building.

The work of each man soon took shape from the character of the person engaged in the effort. Some of the "improvements" were carefully and thoroughly made. Others were makeshifts, many of the settlers, idling away much of their valuable time. In all this the careful and greedy nature of the man who in the last extremity had clung to his gold soon was manifest. He worked as well and faithfully as the rest. Indeed, no one did more, but in order to carry out his plans he occasionally secured help in clearing his land and planting his field from some of the indolent ones, paying them small sums from his store. The money was of little worth, at the time, it being generally understood that only upon the rescue of the company could it have value. And it was upon this supposition only that it was taken. Still, it was found then as it is today, that many men who would not work for themselves made very tolerable and useful servants when under the eye and management of a master. Our "moneyed man," however, paid out but little of his coin, the major portion he kept intact. The little thus placed in circulation being "traded" about from hand to hand much as boys do their balls and tops. It served, however, to keep the minds of the colonists familiar with the idea of money, and to induce them to rate, in their barters and agreements, all their products and services as of so many dollars in value.

Finally, as we have heretofore seen, the hope, and even the desire, of leaving the island having largely disappeared, improvements multiplied and commerce being established, the use of money took on greater force and obtained further power. The desire to accumulate money now seemed to take complete possession of most active and energetic men. Everything that they had they gave to obtain it. In this mad rush for power our greedy friend of the money bags played a prominent part. He now became the great man of the island. Possessing gold he soon perfected a plan, by means of the exaction of interest for its use, which necessitated its return to him. No dollar went out

from his coffers without this "string" being attached to it. With this he pulled it back. The chain was endless. It revolved for him. But the simple colonists chose to remain in ignorance of this, the cause of their undoing.

As a matter of course large numbers of the islanders having pledged their homes to the money dealer lost them. Communication with the rest of the world having been established these homes were sold "on payments" to new comers by Mr. Greedyman, the new owner, who made preparations to "turn an honest penny" by playing with the new crop of home seekers the same game—that of the cat with the mouse. When complaint was made of his doings he promptly proceeded to denounce the complainers as "anarchists," complaining himself in turn that these people spoke evil of "law and order" and the privileges of that "civilization" which had been so hardly obtained by the labors and privations of the early settlers. He often took occasion to remind those who would listen to him there was "just as much money as ever," and that any one could always get money if he would only "work and produce something for sale." Still, many of the islanders contrasted, in their minds, the condition of the people before "civilization" had made its advent with that which prevailed under its sway. And they often wondered in a childish sort of a way how it was that Mr. Greedyman, who had actually produced no more of the wealth of the island than many of the poorer residents, could now be the possessor of a large part of all upon it, simply from the fact that he had brought a bag of coin to shore, which in the early days all had seen was of little use and less value. But that was all—thay only wondered. Meantime the islanders became known in foreign parts as Mr. Greedyman's island. He was often spoken of as the wonderful man; and the real creator of values there. Wealth, it is said, had largely increased; true, most of it was held by him, but then, it had increased and that was something to be thankful for.

"Civilization" was now in full blast upon this island, Mr. Greedyman built railroads, erected gas and water works, and made various improvements, not forgetting to collect in one way and another vast sums in rents, profits and interest, which in cunning ways were fastened upon the foolish people who looked up to him in the precise way in which a certain eminent mammonist desired Jesus to fall down and worship him. But the people forgot the precepts of truth and said among themselves: "Money has always controlled and it always will;" and they made haste among themselves to do him honor.

We can now see that the islanders have arrived at the condition in which we find ourselves today. And we got there just as they did. The islanders under the plea of "progress" and "advancing civilization" were gradually deprived of the natural rights which they originally and rightfully possessed as a gift from the common Father of all. And this is the case with the great body of the American people today.

The French National Assembly was right in its solemn declaration made "in the presence of the Supreme Being and with the hope of his blessing and favor"—Ignorance, neglect or contempt of human rights are the sole causes of public misfortunes and corruptions of government."

Free Soil.

If we go back, in our minds, to the time when the shipwrecked company first landed upon the unknown and uninhabited island we shall be able to see clearly that each one of the company had an undoubted right to use so much of the island and its products as may have been necessary to the support of life in comfort. This was—and is—a natural right. That is, it came from nature and because of the human nature and necessities of the individuals composing the company. Land and its natural products, then, form the provision made by nature—or the Creator—for the use and sustenance of men, of all men, during life. When life is done need ceases, and title, natural title, comes to an end. Natural title, right title, comes simply from the nature of man—from his necessities. His need is his warrant. "Natural opportunities," or the earth in a state of nature, is the answer of God to the need of man. (Right here is the origin and foundation of the now fully received doctrine of the Fatherhood of God and the brotherhood of man.) "All men"—not all governments—"are endowed by their Creator with certain inalienable rights." That is, rights which cannot be alienated or taken away. But suppose this company of people, previous to its advent upon the island, had been reading the book "Progress and Poverty," by Henry George, and had undertaken to deprive the different individuals composing the company of this most important right with which the Creator has endowed "all men," by putting his theories—or the theories of Patrick Edward Dove—into practice. Then, they would say: "This island belongs to this company by right of discovery." "All the land belongs to all the people." Whoever uses the soil must pay to some one representing the company "the full rental value" of the same for the privilege of its use. And he must pay the full rental value, otherwise he secures a privileged position." It is then a matter of entire indifference to the settler whether he cultivates land or not. If he produces food the company fines him for doing so. If he does nothing the authority representing the company is supposed to distribute to him some of the "full rental value' obtained from the foolish fellows who do cultivate. This system is thus seen to fine the workers for working!

The truth is, the right to land is inalienable in the person of the individual, under all ordinary circumstances, and no authority short of that of the Creator has a right to interfere or tax this

ndowment of God; to come, as it were,
between man and the gift of God.
Wherever land is needed for public use
the right of the many to a particular lo-
cality, exceeds that of the one, as a matter of course. This has been illustrated
in the case of "the salt works;" and the
right of the public would be seen in the
building of a wharf by the islanders and
the laying out of a town near by. When
Henry George first began to advocate
the "single tax" he exempted from its
operation a homestead, or a sufficient
portion of the earth's surface for self-
support, thus preserving the natural
right of man. To please the comfortable
classes he afterward dropped this; thus
neglecting the cause of the poor and the
homeless. The justice of exempting
incomes from taxation below a certain
amount is universally recognized. Apply this principle to land and we have
free soil, free homes, a brave and self-
reliant people and the pursuit of happiness made possible. The sufficient answer to the "single tax," as now pre-
sented, is that it circumscribes and denies the inalienable right of man; it
would alienate by taxation, or fine, that
which is inalienable. Our Declaration
of Independence states truly that governments are instituted to preserve these
rights, not to alienate or hinder them.
And the whole course of history proves
that "ignorance, neglect or contempt of
these rights is the sole cause of public
misfortunes and corruptions of government." Beware, in this matter, as in
all others, of those who would deprive
men, for the absolutely certain result is
degradation and eventual despair.
Many men seeing the injustice of the
present land tenures favor the single tax
because, having never fully investigated
the matter, they imagine it the only
remedy—being advocated as it is by able
men. But so is "protection" for Carnegie and Pullman, and other humbugs
too numerous to mention. Let men
think for themselves.

But suppose that after our company
had landed upon the island and partially
"improved" it by the building of houses
and the planting of fields, that a new
company of people arrives, precisely as
the original company did. The first settlers have barely scratched the surface
here and there. There is an abundance
of room for all and the new company is
as destitute as the first. Plainly, the
right of the individuals in the se cond
company is the same as that of those in
the first. To so much of the land as
may have been necessary to their support the first comers had a right. That
is, they had a right to take it, and labor
upon it. Having taken it and labored
upon it they have a right to hold it during life. But they have no right to more
than is absolutely essential to the support of life in comfort. They have no
right, no natural right, no moral right,
to more than they can cultivate properly
by means of their own labor. To allow
a man with a bag of gold to hire others
and monopolize land soon destroys the
natural right of men without gold, as we
have seen. In a previously unknown
and uninhabited island the right of the
second company to choose locations for
themselves on unoccupied land would
be immediately granted. "The natural
and instinctive apprehension of justice
finding universal lodgment in the heart
of man"—where not clouded and ob-
scured by churchianity and so-called civilization—would compel it. The new
company would be welcomed and made
happy, if of the same nationality.
Should any one appear inclined to monopolize land, as did Mr. Greedyman,
taxation forms a legitimate mode of re-
pression. But the idea of securing man's
natural right to apply labor to natural
opportunities for the support of life, by
means of repressive taxation, the proceeds of such taxation to be distributed
equally among idlers as well as workers,
must have originated with the fellow who
holds that the world owes him a living,
whether he labors for it or not. It is
only another device for the robbery of
labor, and it proposes to arrive at its
results in the old fashioned way, by depriving men of their natural rights. In
this connection it would be well to re-

member that wrong never by lapse of time becomes right. Having no just title to the earth's surface, past robbers of men could give none. Our case—the care of the present generation of men—is that of the later comers in the island, and our title is as good, to life and the provision for our support made by our mother nature, as that of the earlier arrivals. But we must labor in some useful capacity. If we refuse, our rights lapse and come to an end. The world owes no man a living who will not work. The right to live we have; the right to apply labor to natural opportunities is given us, then we are to work out our own salvation or perish.

"All that a man hath will he give for his life.' But he cannot live without land. Either he will be a producer of values or a mere dead weight upon the body politic. But even non-producers and paupers have certain rights among men, and with these what is called the land question is closely connected. The right to apply labor to land without the payment of tribute to any, is the most important natural right of man, for the reason that by these means life can always be preserved. By means of it liberty and independence can be maintained and the individual freed from that soul debasing dependence which is so destructive of manhood and character. This is the private and individual right of man. But, as we have seen in the case of "the salt works," men have other claims upon the land which can only be preserved by public action. We have, then, the public and private rights of men as related to natural opportunities. How these may both be preserved has seemed to many a most puzzling question; most of the answers returned being, in fact, a complete surrender of one or the other of these rights. But the question, despite its immense importance, must admit of some plain and simple answer. And this will appear to be the case if we admit fully and freely both the public and private right of men to the soil. Suppose, then, that we adopt as our maxim something like

this—Public things to the public; private affairs to the individual—and seek by legislation to make it operative. To put this in practice, some years ago I proposed and published the following constitutional amendment, not because it is perfect or incapable of amendment, but for the reason that in this way my meaning may be fully explained. Any state may place this in its constitution whenever a majority of its citizens desire, and the powers of the state are ample for its enforcement.

Sec. 1—Real estate and all usual improvements to the value of a sum not exceeding (say three thousand) held, used and occupied in good faith as a home by any usual and private family, is hereby forever exempted from all taxation of every kind and character in this state.

Sec. 2—All lands and natural opportunities needed for public use or business, as certain limited and restricted areas in towns and cities, all mines, forests, waterfalls, or other natural opportunities not available for cultivation, or as dwelling places, are hereby expressly exempted from these provisions.

Sec. 3—The right of every family to the exclusive possession of a homestead held, used and occupied as described in section one, valued at a sum not exceeding (say $3,000) shall not be abridged or denied by any contract, agreement, mortgage or other document, or promise whatsoever, made or executed on or after July 4, 1895.

Sec. 4—The legislature shall have power to pass all laws necessary to carry into effect the due intent and meaning of these provisions.

The constitution of a state or nation is properly a bill of rights. Hence here is the place for the statement of a fundamental right.

There is land enough in the world for all and to spare. The total population of the globe, estimated at 1,400,000,000, could stand upon a plot of ground ten miles square. The single state of Texas with its quarter million square miles could give to every family of five in the whole world, including the millions of India, Africa, China and Japan, a garden spot of more than half an acre in extent. And as not more than half, in any event, would wish to devote their labor to land, this allotment might be nearly doubled in size. Probably the area of land within the United States is at least a hundred times in excess of the actual necessities of the people.

The legislation proposed would not interfere with existing titles or mortgages but would prevent all mortgaging of homes after July 4, 1895. Its effect would probably be mainly as follows: Taxation would increase upon land not held by occupation and used as a home, and upon that portion of estates held in excess of the $3,000 exempted. Increased taxation would gradually decrease the selling price of land and increase the ability of home seekers to purchase. The rush to the cities would cease. The laborer who could profitably employ himself upon a free home which, when once it was his could not be taken from him, would cease to compete with him who might not be able to buy land. Wages would rise. The herding together of vast masses of poverty stricken people in the great cities would be checked and perhaps entirely prevented. Once possessed of a free and inalienable home the citizen would become indeed a king who could not be crushed. The exemption would cover the home of the mechanic or the tradesman in the town, the garden of the vegetable or fruit grower near by and the farm of the farmer at a greater distance. All lands held or used for public or business purposes, as the business portions of towns or cities, could not be held as untaxed homes. If land held as a home were needed for public or business purposes the legislature is empowered to provide means for its acquirement.

Property enough now escapes taxation altogether upon which taxes might be laid sufficient to meet all necessary public expenses. Too much is now raised, and the amount should be decreased. The school system of a state should be under state contro and the state pay all the expenses. The right to occupy and use could be sold precisely as men now sell government "claims." Every facility for making exchanges of this character might be given. Title while in possession shoul t be absolute. Occupancy and use is the only natural title

to land; it is the only defensible title, upon a moral basis. Make it the actual and legal title and the problem is solved. Let us cease to hold up a lie as the foundation of our land laws and man will at last be freed from the consequences of the vast robbery perpetrated by the "robber barons" of old.

But suppose all this to have beee accomplished. It is true that the blank despairing poverty of the present would then be impossible; that men would take heart once more and a race of unconquerable freedom-loving citizens be created and encouraged. But man lives not by bread alone. Mere sustenance for the body is, after all, but little of life. The interchange of thought and the products of labor make civilization possible, and by means of these, true companionship and the association of men together for laudible purposes become possible. These things distinguish the civilized man from the barbarian, and make possible the triumphs of education, art and progress. It is seen that all progress in the past has been secured largely as the result of commerce and exchange of ideas and the products of man's labor. Modern commerce had its origin, almost a thousand years ago, largely from the formation of the Hanseatic League, an organization entered into by a number of the cities of Northern Europe for the purposes of trade. This really broke the long religious night of the "dark ages" and made possible the triumphs of later years. Indeed, one has but to read the history of the past with an unprejudiced eye in order to be convinced that these have been the means employed resulting in the gradual enlightenment of men and the increase of knowledge on the earth.

The second great natural right of man is that of free and untrammeled exchange.

Free Trade, Free Speech, Free Men.

The awful misery of millions of poverty-stricken people cries out against the so-called civilization of our time.

It cries to heaven for relief and justice. Men have forgotten their brothers in the mad scramble for money, and without apparent compunction are engaged in oppressing, depriving and degrading them.

> "See yonder poor, o'erlabored wight,
> So abject, mean and vile,
> Who begs a brother of the earth
> To give him leave to toil;
> And see his lordly fellow worm
> The poor petition spurn,
> Unmindful though a weeping wife
> And helpless offspring mourn."

But a mighty revolution in thought and feeling has at last declared itself in the hearts of many. The pendulum of time has reached the farthest limit. The turning point has been past and nothing can now stay its resistless momentum. The petition of brotherhood has been heard. The duty of man to man is once more discussed. The pendulum of God begins to return. Human sympathy draws it and the power of the Almighty is behind it. Its onward march will be irresistible. A mighty change has already manifested itself in the minds of men. But the immediate outcome may be either joyous or sorrowful. That the result may be happy every true reformer should exert his utmost power to prevent the adoption by the wronged and suffering people of unlawful and revengeful methods. He who cries out against wrong must do no wrong. Whoever demands justice must do no injustice. Failing in this the end may be told from the beginning. Past history shows it. A military despotism is the certain end and inevitable result. Patience, then, my brothers; the mills of the gods grind slowly but they grind exceedingly fine.

In the revolution of 1848, which shook all Europe from center to circumference, the mistake was made which must not be repeated. "At that time we had all Europe at our feet," said a most intelligent German to me some years ago, "but we did not know how to use our victory; excesses were committed which turned the middle classes against us. Our leaders were divided in their councils. They were successful in tearing down, but they knew not how to build. Upon no plan or principle were they agreed."

Now, today, the old is passing away. The new will take its place. What shall it be? Unification of thought among reformers is a paramount necessity. We must know what we want and agree upon it. Upon this all true progress waits. I have endeavored to trace, in an exceedingly hurried manner it is true, the course by which we as a people have lost some of the freedom of the past, and by means of which we stand in deadly peril of losing more. I have shown that the course taken by the controllers of events in this country has led to the deprivation of the great masses of the people, and that degredation follows hard after.

That the wealthy and powerful through political methods have deprived and are depriving men of those natural and God-given rights upon which all true liberty rests and depends. And this matter of natural right no one need take my word as a guide. I but repeat the words of the wise and the true of all ages.

Think, my brother, for one moment, clearly and candidly for yourself. Do you imagine for an instant that men may be deprived of what the Creator has intended for freemen and that they may still retain freedom? Was that grand declaration of our fathers mere idle bombast? Have men no natural rights? Were they placed upon this rolling ball to be the mere serfs and tools of their more crafty brothers? And will you be a slave? If so, witness all about you the daily forging of your chains.

The crisis is upon us! And the foundations of the future upon which true and brave men must build is plain. The natural rights of men upon the earth, with which they have been endowed by a beneficent Creator, must be secured and preserved to all, both high and low, great and small.

"The principles of Jefferson are the definitions of free society * * * This is a world of com

pensations and he who would be no slave must
consent to have no slave Those who deny
freedom to others deserve it not for themselves
and under God they cannot long retain it."—
Abraham Lincoln

Wherever monopoly rears its crested
head the public must take it in charge.
Public things to the public; private affairs to the individual. Money, rail-
ways and the telegraph, must be nation-
alized, as is the case with the post-
office. Free homes for the people and
free exchange of products of the toil of
both hand and brain will bring the rest.

Protection? True protection for the
industries of the country can be had in
but one way. National paper money
will secure it- Absolute money, unre-
deemable in gold, this is the touchstone
of industrial freedom; this will protect
the manufacturer and protect the laborer.

Not good? Not good unless exchanged
for gold? Full legal tender money is a
legal decree backed by the sovereign
power of the nation. Not good? It is as
good and of as powerful a nature as the
nation that issues it. No less and no
more. As well say that the decree of a
court co veying property from one
claimant to another is not good unless
engraved on gold intrinsically as valuable as the property conveyed! Bosh!
Where are the brains and reasoning
powers of men that they are deceived by
so transparent a lie? Not good? Your
enemies, the enemies of labor, the enemies of humanity, the enemies of God—
the Jew gold brokers of New York and
London—know perfectly well that such
money is good; and further, they know
that such money will liberate the world
from their clutches. For this reason
they fight and affect to scorn it. Ridi-
cule is a powerful weapon. Hence they
make use of it in their hired presses and
by the hired mouths of their lackeys
and tools. But fear is the controlling
motive. They fear that men may learn
the truth—and practice it.

Suppose only national legal tender
money, receivable for all dues and debts
to be used. Then, if goods are brought
this country from abroad they could

be exchanged for this money or for the
products of the country. If this money
is taken in exchange it must be ex-
pended here. Thus production is stim-
ulated and demand for our goods increased. Every shipment of goods
brought in makes demand for an equal
amount of our products. The more
goods sent here from abroad the greater
the demand upon our labor. Fair and
free exchange is mutually beneficial.
But if money redeemable in gold is used
in commerce the people having the
cheapest labor and the heaviest loanable
capital soon relieve the other of their
gold; take away their money, deprive
them of the principal tool of trade; impoverish them. This is why both Old
and New England are so strenuously for
"a gold basis." By means of this jug-
glery millions of people and many nations have been victimized and impov-
erished. And the money changers did
it. They will impoverish us in the same
way unless we, the people, get our eyes
open to the gambling game that is being
played. Our money lords understand
all this well, and are already preparing
to emigrate to "perfidious Albion,"
where their perfidy is fully known.

Free trade is not to blame. Gold basis
money is. But the crafty dealers in gold
make the foolish people think that the
result of their deviltry—the present de-
pression—comes from a fear of a free
exchange of goods.

They cry "tariff." But the cry is only
intended to divert attention from the
misdeeds of the money changers. Commerce is not to blame. The money
changers are. Money is a common
carrier of values. And as a common
carrier it should be at the command of
whoever has value to carry in trade.
Afraid of free trade! Think for a moment what that means. And if not
afraid of your own freedom in this matter why should you seek to limit the
equal freedom of others? "He that
would be no slave must consent to have
no slave." As a common carrier money
should be controlled by the nation for
the common good. Otherwise trade,

commerce, exchange, is subject to the hindrances, ("We can't let you have the money") the charges, ("two per cent a month; money is scarce"), and the impositions, ("We foreclose tomorrow") of the dealers in money. Trade should be free. If not free then the men who would trade are not free. They are deprived of a right, and poverty and degradation is the sure end and result. Trade and commerce to blame for the scarcity of money? What nonsense. But scarcity of money is to blame for the absence of trade. An issue of legal tender greenbacks paid out for government expenses and in lieu of taxation, would revive as by magic the drooping industries of the nation and for the time liberate the industrial masses from economic slavery. And everybody knows it. Hence the opposition of the controllers—the "cornerers"—of money.

"The slightest modification of national laws concerning money affects every branch of trade, every industry, every investment; yet a small number of the whole people, those whose business it is to deal in money, as lenders or bankers, alone keep that close watch of legislation which enables them to control it unduly, so as to promote their own interests when laws are changed, or, if laws are likely to affect their interests injuriously they are the first to be aware of the effects of changes, and to guard against them. That prosperity or adversity may result to the majority of an entire people by a simple act of legislation on money with a rapidity that legislation on no other subject can parallel, has become obvious to all intelligent people.—Chambers Encyclopedia, vol. 10, p. 126.

These are facts. This is the truth. Most intelligent men freely acknowledge it, but stand dumb in the presence of overwhelming injustice. What will rouse them? God only knows. But of this be sure: If they look calmly on while their brothers and sisters perish a worse fate awaits them. It is only delayed for a time.

—They are slaves who fear to speak
For the fallen and the weak;
They are slaves who will not choose
Hatred, scoffing and abuse,
Rather than in silence shrink
From the truth they needs must think.
They are slaves who dare not be
In the right with two or three.
                    —James Russell Lowell.

Every man lives in his thoughts. "As a man thinketh so is he." That he may be a true man he must think truly; he must be able to hear the truth. Truth must be given at least an equal chance with error. Now, men are daily fed with lies upon economic subjects in the great newspapers and from prominent platforms. Lies that are known to be lies by the utterer .

But no man can breathe and ponder a lie and remain unharmed. Speech and the communication of thought must be free from the oppressive hands of the corruptors of our politics. The avenues of information open to the average individual are freighted with lies. The telegraph and the daily press are used chiefly to amuse and deceive. In the latter days of the Roman empire the mob cried out for "Bread and circuses." Our populace, too, is in the process of degradation. Under the baneful influence of the times the masses of the people run hither and thither, "pleased by a rattle and tickled by a straw.' The lies of the daily press they devour. Its hates they absorb. Its toadyings to the rich and the powerful they emulate. Deprived and degraded they lick the hand that smites them. Despised by the men who use them they are to be pitied and helped—liberated. How? By flattery? By telling them of their intelligence and manly virtue? No! But by showing them the truth.

They are what they are because deprived of the truth. As of old, "My people perish for lack of knowledge." Already a great railway company has issued its edict that its employes must abstain from politics. They must not think: or thinking must not speak their thoughts. Free speech is circumscribed and will shortly be denied. The main avenues of information, as is well known, are in the hands of those who mean no good to the people's cause, and yet these are the sources of knowledge to which the people vainly look for light. The wealthy and most corrupt owners of the telegraph have become the real schoolmasters of the nation, and they are educating it away from the truth and in the direction of national dishonor and decay. The telegraph and all the means of communication should be freed from the crafty fingers of these vile manipulators. Like the post-office it should be made the servant and not the master of men.

Free soil, free trade, and free speech make free men! Let us have them all by the restoration to "all men" of those natural rights wherewith the world Creator has endowed them. And who so denies one or all of these rights, let him be known as a depriver and would-be degrader of his kind, an enemy of his brothers and a defier of God.

My brother, we are at the parting of the ways. The past is gone. It will never return. The new is before us. Will you join with us in the effort to better the conditions surrounding poor humanity? Crude and unfinished, it may be, are our efforts, but a mighty earnestness in behalf of the truth, in behalf of suffering men, pervades our ranks and inspires our hearts. We are not perfect. Our knowledge is far from complete. But we desire to know the truth, for the truth shall make us free. Come with us. The morning light is breaking; a new day is dawning upon men; a day in which justice shall be done and in which no man shall be oppressed. Comrade! give us your hand and your aid in the fight.

(The end.)

www.ingramcontent.com/pod-product-compliance
Lightning Source LLC
Chambersburg PA
CBHW021549270326
41930CB00008B/1432